4017 43

BANGKOK DAYS

LAWRENCE OSBORNE

NORTH POINT PRESS
A DIVISION OF FARRAR, STRAUS AND GIROUX
NEW YORK

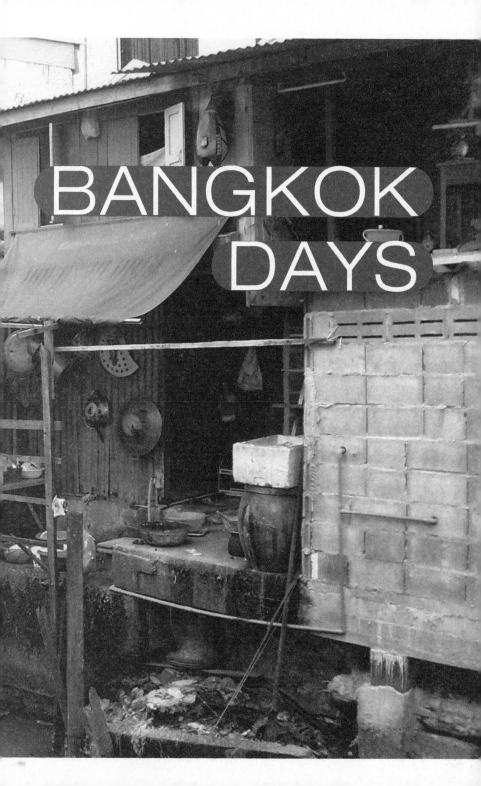

BANGKOK DAYS

North Point Press
A division of Farrar, Straus and Giroux
18 West 18th Street, New York 10011

Copyright © 2009 by Lawrence Osborne
All rights reserved
Distributed in Canada by Douglas & McIntyre Ltd.
Printed in the United States of America
First edition, 2009

Library of Congress Cataloging-in-Publication Data
Osborne, Lawrence, 1958–
    Bangkok days / Lawrence Osborne.— 1st ed.
        p.   cm.
    ISBN-13: 978-0-86547-732-2 (hardcover : alk. paper)
    ISBN-10: 0-86547-732-9 (hardcover : alk. paper)
    1. Bangkok (Thailand)—Description and travel.   2. Osborne,
Lawrence, 1958– —Travel—Thailand—Bangkok.   I. Title.

DS589.B2O65 2009
915.93—dc22
[B]

                                                    2008044741

Designed by Jonathan D. Lippincott

www.fsgbooks.com

        1   2   3   4   5   6   7   8   9   10

For Chris and Sam
Many fêtes

CONTENTS

The names of businesses in Bangkok change as fast as they do anywhere else. I have, in general, kept names from years past wherever appropriate, though many will have disappeared. All names of individuals have been altered for privacy's sake.

Needless to say, this is not a study of Thai culture, and all mistakes in its interpretation are my own.

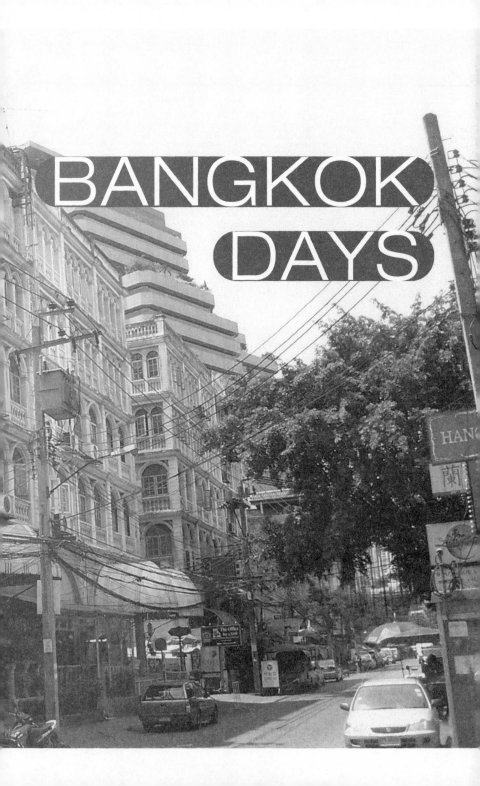

All lust is grief.
—*Buddhist proverb*

A few years ago I lived in a neighborhood called Wang Lang. From where I sit now, watching trains cross to Manhattan on the Brooklyn Bridge, my river balcony in Bangkok seems like a patch of paradise forever lost. Disassembled and stowed away in a hopeless corner of the mind, where it's bound to rot. At this very hour, when New York seems filled with threatening drama and artificial colors, the Chao Phraya River is filled with gentle monks bobbing around on water taxis. The two cities couldn't be more different. There, saffron is the color of dusk. The river brings peace. The monks got off at Wang Lang pier with their umbrellas and mala rosaries, which traditionally contain 108 beads for the 108 passions of men enumerated by Avalokiteshvara. They looked up at the *farang* drinking his gin and tonic on the balcony, and that look contained both amusement and distance as it asked, "Is that a lonely man?" The look of Buddha as he extends protection with his left hand raised, *abhaya.*

I preferred nights there. The days were too hot and I like heat only when there's no sun. I was a night walker. It is a loneliness which has been chosen and indeed calculated. I spent the small hours on the streets, marauding like a raccoon. I grew to like the atmosphere of stale basil and exhausted marijuana which Bangkok seemed to breathe out of invisible nostrils; I liked the girls who spin past you in the dark with the words *"Bai nai?"* like coins that have been flipped in a bar. I liked the furious rot.

I woke up from a siesta in a small white room in the apartment complex called Primrose Apartments. I didn't keep much there. A cut-price Buddha from the Chatuchak market, a bookshelf. I had a carpet from India, too. When you are broke, life is simple. I made myself a gin and tonic on the balcony and waved to the monks. The days were empty by design. I didn't have a job; I was on the lam, as old American gangsters had it. A perfect phrase. The lam. It means "headlong flight," according to my Webster's dictionary. Lamming, *to run away.*

Across the hallway lived an Englishman called McGinnis. I wondered if that was a real name, or whether it was a borrowed one. He had an air of upper-class twittery, with his polelike physique stripped of muscle and his linen whites which had missed their era by a wide mark. McGinnis sold air-conditioning systems to Bangkok conference centers and hotels, a profitable business in sweltering Bangkok, and after-hours he said he was compiling an encyclopedia of bars to enrich the lives of others. He looked like a dirty cat at that hour, and I'd see him sitting on his balcony, slowly drinking a Singha mixed with some kind of fruit cordial and eating olives. He looked me in the eye and smiled, as if stroking a cat as well as being one. On the other side was a Spaniard called Helix. Helix—not Felix? I thought I'd heard him correctly. Helix the painter, who painted frescoes behind bars in Bangkok conference centers and hotels. They were typical of the profound, talented men you find in Bangkok.

There were others. On the ground floor lived another expat, an older Scot called Farlo who ran a holiday lodge which he had built himself for adventurous types, in Cambodia. He was a former British Army paratrooper from Dundee, and he wore a beret on the side of his head. Inside that head was lodged a piece of shrapnel from the war in Angola. Cuban shrapnel. You didn't want to cross him drunk in the corridor at night. He'd grab your arm and say, "It's time for a wank, son."

At six every night I went down to the street, feeling very much like John Wilmot, earl of Rochester, perfumed from a cold shower. The Primrose opened directly into the street, the way that an elevator opens directly into a penthouse.

Wang Lang is a pandemonious place in a pandemonious city. Its main drag is so narrow you can feel both sides of it brushing against your hips as you walk through it. As I went sweating between the open kitchens, I was followed by children jeering, *"Yak farang, yak farang!"* (foreign giant). I was the largest human there, a phenomenon in their eyes, and perhaps worse than that, a genetic accident which couldn't be reversed.

It was a hospitable place for a man who has done nothing, and who will probably never do anything. For someone with no career, with no prospects, permanently broke, it was the perfect asylum. Its gold-tinted eggs and its bags of oolong tea were virtually free. One could graze continuously on delicasies one had never heard of and still be in pocket. It was well suited to a lazy cunt, in other words, and a natural habitat for a man on the lam who had no objective in his day-to-day life but an inquisitive loitering, a selfless promenading for its own sake. A man who has turned into a ruminant, a goat.

•

In Wang Lang I perfected that Thai style of eating on the run called *khong kin len*, where you pile different ingredients onto a banana leaf as you sail along, walking and pondering at the same time, never losing balance. The streets are cul-de-sacs, so there is no point in having a direction. They all end in little theaters and cafés by the water.

And so I found myself walking up and down, eating those gilded eggs and bits of dried squid, and as night fell the air went ash-gray and the nostrils opened to greet something indefinable, the pungency of "mouse shit" chilies being tossed in hot oil and tamarind paste, and I began to sink like a stone into my own well. The city is nothing more than a protocol for this sinking. Because Bangkok is where some people go when they feel that they can no longer be loved, when they give up.

It was also true of the other tenants. Broken, disappointed, rejected, they had headed east. During my first nights in Wang Lang I played chess with them in the common room, interested by their dazed, suntanned faces. My most favored, however, was McGinnis. He was a man with no past, a character in a Simenon novel who walks out of his house one day, gets on a train, and kills someone in a distant city. He was from Newhaven. "There's nothing in Newhaven," McGinnis would say, "except sea fortifications," and his face was like that of a pleasant hoodlum who has just shot down a kite. Sea fortifications, I would think: but that's a lot. His head was shaved like a soldier's, like Farlo's, but he was nothing of the sort, with his willowy, elongated frame. He was an engineer with a degree in air-conditioning. It's a subject you can get a degree in. He had acquired his in Sheffield.

McGinnis was six foot seven. He towered in doorways, in hotel lobbies, in the light of streetlamps. There was something wonderfully sinister there, and I love sinister men. A sinister man doesn't just walk down a street, he rolls down it like a superior ball bearing. A sinister man cannot be amiable, but he can be good company. Despite his association with the science of air-conditioning, McGinnis was also subtly aristocratic and refined, while doing nothing better with his life than selling mass-produced cooling units. It was okay with him. There are aristocrats of the spirit who are mundane in their daily lives. Everything about him was happily self-contained, replete. Is this what made him sinister?

It was hotter than usual around Christmastime. In the supermarkets, choirs of girls in red velvet dresses swung brass bells in fur-trimmed hats and chimed out the words to "Silent Night" and "Jingle Bells." The tofu bars had sprigs of plastic holly on them and yuletide slogans crisscrossed the steaming skycrapers of a Buddhist city. The days were windless, our river surged past the Primrose, sloppy and violent, the color of pea soup into which a baby has puked. Its surface was thickened by strands of aquatic weed, and on the far bank the city temples rose like huge stalagmites, or legumes with bristling skins. Somerset Maugham, one of the few Western writers to describe Bangkok in detail, says somewhere that one should be grateful that "something so fantastical exists."

•

Something stirred within me whenever I took my coffee on the balcony in the morning and inhaled the river stench of gasoline and mud. As if a dead leaf on the floor of me were suddenly being lifted and flipped with a small sound, a scratching of dead matter coming to life again. A pricking of the inner lining of the gut. I watched the rice barges crashing toward Klong Tuey port, the gossiping monks with their umbrellas and briefcases ferrying back and forth from those same temples strung out along the river. And behind them the four gold towers of the Royal Palace and, more distantly, Wat Arun sparkling with reflections from a million fragments of glass and ceramic rosebuds, with the sugary ornament of the Italian craftsmen who fashioned them two and a half centuries ago. Monks and schoolchildren in navy blazers, and the men operating the boats blowing ear-splitting whistles as they swept up to the pier. As the tires slung along the boat struck the rotting wood, there was a delicious sound: *phuck*.

From here I saw McGinnis doing yoga on his balcony in a jumpsuit, his body elongated to its full length and a trickle of Khmer music coming out of the sliding doors. It was impossible to avoid the other renters at the Primrose because we were always thrust together by the lack of space. He stayed in his yoga position and called over, in his long-exiled accent, "I hear a Spanish guy moved in downstairs the same time as you. He says his name's Helix. Not Felix, *Helix*." And he laughed scornfully.

Before long, McGinnis was taking me downriver on the water taxis to the Oriental Hotel. He dressed up for these river rides, a straw hat and two-tone Loake shoes with steel caps. The *Death in Venice* look. He spoke to schoolgirls in appalling, salacious Thai. The hotel has its own pier, and we jumped off there with all the fat tourists.

"I can understand," he said, "you not having a salary and all."

One sometimes starts explaining oneself immediately to someone one has just met. I seem to have the knack for triggering this reaction. I started coming to Bangkok, I said, in order to get dental care, because I couldn't afford the insurance in New York. It was as simple as that. Fourteen cavities and a root canal cost me $450 in Bangkok, which was a fraction of my yearly insurance premium. Even with the airfare and a month's rent at the Primrose, I was in pocket. My whole rationale for being there, in fact, was financial. It was money that governed my temporary exile, for the math was clear-cut: the West was now far too expensive. With time, I was coming closer to the idea that I might have to find somewhere like this to live on a permanent basis. In Thailand, I was in pocket most of the time.

"Is that what you say? *In pocket?*"

He laughed.

"Did you have your teeth done this time?"

"I am waiting for a check."

"Oh, you're waiting for a check!"

•

McGinnis took me to the Bamboo Bar. He took out a mechanical toy and placed it on the bar. It was a Brazilian tree frog made of wood, and it chattered on a spring if you pushed a button. He left it there. "Sooner or later," he said, "some beautiful woman always comes up and asks me what the frog is. And then I tell her."

"What is it?"

"I'll tell you later."

The decor of the Bamboo is rattan and lacquer, for the word "colonial" has nothing but positive connotations in Asia these days, and everything colonial is deemed handsome, stylish. The Bamboo Bar is the most touristy bar in the city, so touristy that it seems to wink at itself, so it is also the most colonial. But since everything is touristy anyway why not direct yourself to the wellhead of the poison and enjoy?

When I came here with McGinnis we were always surrounded by commotion. People came up to him and kissed him, shook my hand, and announced themselves as members of the professions that dominate Bangkok: fashion, design, finance, and food. When I came alone, however, the place always seemed to be empty and I passed hours watching *farang* women doing laps in the swimming pool.

When I was alone, I wandered the hotel. There was usually a string quartet in a lobby that was animated without being animate. Too many of the rich, scurrying about with their hands full, too many bellhops, too many Japanese matrons in white gloves playing cards.

I took the underground corridors deep inside the hotel where you could see streams bubbling over beds of pebbles, past the windows of Burberry. In the Authors Wing there was a white summerhouse atrium and a staircase leading up to the suites named after the writers that all Asian hotel suites are named after: Conrad, Maugham, Agatha Christie.

There was no Jeffrey Archer suite yet, but in the library there was a portrait of the great novelist as Lord of Weston-super-Mare. I sat by the grandfather clock and read Evelyn Waugh's *A Tourist in Africa*. "No one ever made a servant of a Masai," Waugh wrote of his journey through Kenya in 1959. It's a mysterious sentence. To walk for the sake of walking—the most aimless thing of all—reminds us why the Masai cannot be servants: they are nomads.

McGinnis stopped his chattering frog and said, "Long before you came here I was in the same predicament. I wanted a place I could wander about in and where nothing would add up. European cities were too familiar. American cities were too like European ones. I wanted a city with no streets. A script I couldn't read. Total oblivion."

One night recently, he said, he had heard a curious sound coming from the Spaniard's apartment. When he turned off the radio and went down the stairs to investigate, he could tell that it was the Spaniard's voice. It repeated a single word over and over, and it was almost in a scream.

"He was shouting *mierda, mierda!*"

"What do you make of that?"

He went to the window of the Spaniard's apartment, which wasn't in the least curtained or shuttered. You could look right in.

"The Spaniard was in his underpants in front of a large canvas slathered with glue. He held a dead pigeon in one hand, which he appeared to be in the act of hurling at the canvas. I noticed at once that there were other dead pigeons already pinned to its surface. I realized then that he must have collected them from the streets nearby, which, as I am sure you have noticed, are fairly awash with dead birds of all descriptions. Pigeons, macaws, crows. I have even seen the occasional parrot. In any case, he had decided to make art out of everyday life."

"Isn't that the definition of *mierda*?"

"Yes. And it would be better not to make anything at all. To just go walking."

"I walk at night," I reminded him. "I go everywhere."

"I'll bet you haven't been to the Woodlands Inn."

When a foreigner moves into a city he doesn't understand, he prides himself on acquiring an esoteric knowledge of its hidden crannies. He thinks he is the only one to know a certain tiny bar or an ancient mango tree standing by a canal hidden behind a laundry. Why do these things matter so much to him? Does he really think he is the only one who has noticed them?

•

Next to the Oriental runs the oldest road in Bangkok, Charung Krung, which of course means "New Road" in Thai. It used to be an elephant track running parallel to the river, but for McGinnis, it was a horizontal greased rope along which he could slither after twenty drinks at the Bamboo Bar. There were no whores, no massage parlors, but there was a disreputable motel frequented by Indian doctors where we could get a Cambodian brandy, and they had a Ping-Pong table.

Woodlands Inn was on Charung Soi 32, with 300-baht-an-hour rooms and an Indian restaurant full of cow-eyed crooks. It smelled of condoms and ghee. And who, I wondered, ran the Dr. Manoj Clinic and the Memon Clinic next to it, all those dingy abortion clinics assembled inside the same courtyard as the Woodlands? Who used this corner of a city of ten million, darting in and out of its cubicles? The Indians were all playing backgammon. There was no Cambodian brandy.

"But I had it last time!" the Englishman shouted.

"It is not existing. Royal Stag Indian whiskey we are having."

They began to play some sad Calcutta music, and the old men sang along, their eyes croony and wet. It was a mood. We sat outside on a bench, surrounded by the hollow music of cicadas hanging from the telephone cables, and McGinnis said, "Those cables. Have you noticed that every street has these masses of tangled cables? It's because the telephone company never replaces or takes down cables that have ceased functioning. They simply add new ones, ad nauseam. Eventually the cables will take over the city. I think of them as a life-form, possibly predatory."

At the corner of Charung Krung, the cables were bunched into ancient clusters that were beginning to droop downward to head level, like an infestation of metal wisteria. The city's infuriating topography isn't a rational system at all, it isn't European, it isn't anything one can seize. Near Soi 32—*soi* is the Thai word for a small street—Chinese jewelers and antiquarians sweltered below the cables, Yoo Lim and Thong Thai, and after them came landmarks that my eye had learned to pick out after seeing them a couple of times: the slim neoclassical building housing the Express Light company with its sooted Corinthian capitals, a bright sign for A.A. Philatelic. But it was all flattened in the eye.

McGinnis got up. His immense size caused the Indians to fall silent. The heat made his face glisten and his hair stuck up in greasy tufts. His Gulati suit was now wrinkled and he said he wanted to show me something beautiful, "something beautiful," as he said, "in an ugly city."

MEN WITHOUT WOMEN

As we entered the Muslim neighborhood around the Haroun
Mosque, McGinnis told me about the air-conditioning business, which was technically intricate and, like all things intricate for a good reason, fascinating. Refrigeration itself
seemed so much more convincing than writing articles for a
living. It had a point: it improved people's lives, even though
it damaged the ozone layer. It made the world colder, which
is never a bad thing.

So when he asked what I was doing, I said, "I'm treading
water." Tactfully, he let it go at that because it is understood
among the full-time lammers that Bangkok is an asylum for
those who have lapsed into dilettantism, as one might lapse
into a temporary period of mental instability. The great projects, the ambitious flights of the mind—all trashed. They
might revive, but not now.

This idleness enters the movements of the body. One
loses electrical fire and nervosity. Even the hands and feet
become languid. So we talked instead about sex, in empty
Muslim alleys where there was none. Hadn't Buddhist Bangkok quietly accepted its role as the provider of sexual services to the rest of the planet? In a global economy it was
inevitable that some place would. But what did that tell you
about the rest of the world?

Men can talk for hours about sex, but they don't know
what it is exactly they are discussing. It is a lacuna, not a

real subject. They edge their way around a slipping vacuum, because they are investigating not sex but women, and women are sometimes a lacuna in their minds where there should be something solid. But when they are in Bangkok, they converse about it with greater intensity, because their own women are no longer present, nor even at the edges of their field of vision. They are in a place where they can behave like gay men, where their masculinity is condensed, intensified.

We inspected the mosque and McGinnis knew all its history, from the time of its founding by an Indonesian immigrant in 1928. It was partially colored like a chocolate egg, and so light in construction that its wood could have been mistaken for paper. Lean and tattered, McGinnis seemed so perfectly adapted to this context that one had to wonder how much of his time he spent nosing around these dead-end streets, history books in hand. There are men like the walking books in *Fahrenheit 451* who are content to pass their lives slowly filling up with knowledge which can never be used, and it is the very filling up that gives them a sense of life's pointless sweetness.

"It may be," he said, taking off his glasses and rubbing them with the German-made Brillen-Putztücher wipes he carried with him at all times, "that this is the one building in Bangkok that lasts a thousand years, because nobody will bother with it."

•

We rolled a joint and smoked it with the deliberation of two old men sharing a bottle of wine. I noticed for the first time the fine white scars on McGinnis's cheeks, like the tracks of

skates on fresh ice. A childhood disease, a brush with a croc-
odile or a filariasis worm, a sign from the beyond? It made
his square, military head look morbidly dashing, as if they
were saber wounds. He had done two years at Sandhurst,
after all. He had fencer's hands.

"I have wondered," he drawled, "if we could invent a
new word for cock? I have considered Sí Señora, already
much used in Latin America. Or Roger the Dodger."

"Then cunt would be Sí Señor?"

"Precisely. But I like 'cunt.' 'Cunt' is a lovely word. A
noble word."

It goes back to John Wilmot, he said, and even further,
to the Domesday Book, where it wasn't mentioned, to
Edward the Confessor, and maybe even to the Venerable
Bede.

"The Venerable Bede said 'cunt'?"

"He would have said *cynt*. That's the Anglo-Saxon. In
Chaucer it's pronounced *queynte*. A word that also meant
cunning. The word 'cunt,' in fact, is unfairly vilified. A man
who genuinely loves women doesn't trawl the streets at night
thinking, 'I wish I could get some *vagina* tonight.' Not at
all, he thinks, *I want some cunt*. I can't understand why
a woman would be with someone who uses the word
"vagina" in his internal monologues. It just means 'recepta-
cle' in Latin. *The Vagina Monologues*? I'd rather have *The
Cunt Dialogues*. 'Cunt' comes from the Indo-European root
ku, a word associated with both femininity and knowledge."

"By the way," he added, "have you noticed that whenever you type 'cunt' into a Microsoft Word document it
underlines it in red as an unknown word? That's underground power."

We came to windows through which we could see whole families on their bellies gathered around three-inch TV sets, among saucers of cardamom and piles of comics, the thresholds lined with cloth slippers. The houses were yellow and turquoise behind metal screens, with steeply angled gardens packed with fruit trees and shielded by graceful wooden doors painted fir-green and red. Such places are rare in Bangkok, remains of an old city that few can now remember and which are now being plowed under in a prolonged fit of amnesia. In them one's conversation with the past resumes so that one falls silent even in company and walks like a street cat, guided by the night retina.

Along one side of this neighborhood and close to the water stands a square Italian villa decorated with weed trees, decayed into a living ruin: the old Customs House known as Khong Phasi, now the Bang Rak fire station. Within a lunette carved from the façade is a woman's face, turned to one side, smiling like someone waving goodbye from a train window. She is carefully individuated, a face out of the past and delicately set as a blancmange.

From the firehouse an alley called Trok Rong Phasi ran back to the French Embassy, and the shadows of summery trees lay across it. We turned and drank in this fermenting ruin, constructed by an exiled Italian engineer in 1892 as a memory of the ruined street corners of Genoa, which he must have missed.

"That's what I wanted to show you," McGinnis said, nodding at the lunette and the woman's head. "He was clearly inspired by a Della Robbia in Florence, wouldn't you say?"

I went frequently to Trok Rong Phasi by myself after

that, learning the way its alleys intersected, and finding that they formed a beautiful pattern like a torn spiderweb. On occasion I got an ice cream and paused by the massive gates of the French Embassy with its twin lamps, looking up at the sweep of a nineteenth-century terrace where women in baking crinolines must once have taken the river air.

In the waterside café, a group of Scandinavian girls had gathered under the parasols, pink as crayfish in that dust-tinged light. They talked so loudly we could hear the gaps between their sentences. On the part of the property that faced the water, an Australian renter named Dennis was seated in front of an easel, picking at a watercolor. I had never seen him before so openly revealed in the sun, an elderly man with skin as white as fine library dust, with a fop of dyed blond hair falling between his eyes, as it must have all his life. I remember thinking, "Women must have loved that fop of hair," and wondering who he really was. A retiree, the others said, who liked the Thai girls. Wife dead, keeps to himself. When I went over to have a look at his watercolor, he didn't say "G'day, mate," but "Good afternoon," and I saw that his painting was an exact replica of the far side of the river. He put on a pair of incredibly frail spectacles and finally dipped his brush into a pot of water. I could hear him thinking in the gloom, "Another useful day completed in the great annals of aimlessness."

"Have you met that Spaniard?" he said as we sat on the pier, looking at the Nordics. "A terrible painter."

"I'm avoiding him for the moment."

"They say he did a mural in Bumrungrad Hospital. In the Italian restaurant there. I went in there one day when I was having a checkup and had a look."

"And?"

"It's called the Portofino. It's fine dining for the invalids. I went into the bar and got myself a martini just to look at his work. I'm curious, I'm a painter too, as you can see. Not a pro, but I like it all the same."

He was a bit like my grandfather, a man whom I had adored. An amateur scholar of sorts. He got up and said, "Come and have a beer with me on the terrace."

From there, we looked down at the Primrose.

"Cheap and comfy at least," he said sadly. "Cheap and comfy for the masses, dear."

He was reedy and awkward, tensile, with big popping hand veins, and he wore a woodcutter shirt day after day. Retired bank manager. He came here half the year. He spent the other half in Perth.

"Horrible place, Perth. Bangkok's where you find your youth again."

I said that I hadn't found mine.

"You're not sixty yet. Come back when you're sixty."

"I won't be coming here when I'm sixty."

"There are worse places in which to be sixty."

He added that what Bangkok offered to the aging human was a culture of complete physicality. It was tactile, humans pressing against each other in healing heat: the massage, the bath, the foot therapy, the handjob, you name it. The physical isolation and sterility of Western life, its physical boredom, was unimaginable.

"There's a reason we're so neurotic and violent and unhappy. Especially as we get on a bit, no one *ever touches us*."

I thought of him returning from work every evening to a

neat suburban house in Perth, until the day his wife died
and everything came unstuck. Twenty years of not being
touched? That was the way it had been, but one couldn't say
it. The forlorn rags of growing old, or a last beautiful disgrace in the Land of Smiles. He had taken the arduous leap
into the latter. But I wanted to know about the mural in
Bumrungrad Hospital.

"I got myself a martini at the bar. The mural is behind
all the bottles. They have some damn good aged scotches
there. It's a Thai hospital after all. Then there was this mad
painting. I think it showed Christ turning up at a drinking
party of Alexander the Great. I could see the Greeks in their
tunics anyway, and there was the Savior, looking bloody
liquored up. And there was Saint Peter, I think, swigging
from a bottle of Gordon's. It was all very strange. But I
knew it was good for that Spaniard to have painted. He did
a frightful caca for the Shangri-La Hotel over there. I know
that for a fact. What they call an absterraction."

And he pointed at the Shangri-La, far downriver.

"Did you ask the Spaniard himself?"

"One doesn't talk to Spaniards, mate. They're all crackers. I've been wondering, in fact, where all these Latins have
come from. You seem like a nice young man. I wouldn't talk
to the rest of them, if I were you. They seem like a bunch of
skunks to me. I wouldn't touch them with a shitty stick.
Especially that McGinnis. He's got the air of a right little
schnauzer."

He used the word literally.

"Do you paint in Perth?" I asked.

"Crocs, the beach, sunsets. You name it, I paint it."

We admired the breadth and pugnacity of the river. Its

waves crashed noisily against the pier. A river with waves. It was our kind of river, a real bitch of a river.

A water taxi drew up and a nubile girl in a black two-piece suit jumped off. Dennis got to his feet at once and began waving.

"Over'ere, Porntit!"

She looked up and I felt a stab of jealousy.

Dennis sat down again.

"Mate, you got to love a country where Porntit is a real name."

In fact, the name is *Porntip*.

•

Through my windows poured all the noise of Wang Lang. Blindfolded, you would think it was a waterfall, a cataract striking beds of smooth stones. At the corner, blind *wikipo* musicians played *kuen* pipes and an old woman cried out her guts into a microphone. A few *luuk thung* country songs, the bittersweet music of Thailand's rural misery.

I got up at four, put on sandals, and wandered down to the ferry. The monks came off the boats in a swarm, reeking of God. Standing by this part of the river, you have the partial illusion of being in an old city; the embankments are filled with rotting warehouses in that economical Sino-Thai "row house" style known as *hong taew*. After a few days I noticed that Porntip arrived at the pier at the same time every day. She had a quick eye for *farang*s and she made it her business to catch mine as she came up the jetty, swinging a fake Fendi bag. This eye-play is at the core of the city's erotic juggling of East and West. She was not always with Dennis, and I sometimes caught her walking through the premises as if at a loose end, simply dressed in jeans and tank top, looking like one of the students from the universities, which is what she was. She would knock on doors, the rap echoing down the cement corridors, and there was something brittle and excessively polite about that knock. Presumably she didn't need to say anything. When it happened to me, she didn't bother opening a conversation, she stepped into the corridor of my unit smelling of pharmaceutically processed alpine flowers. She didn't mention money. She walked in, tossed off her shoes, and asked me if I had any orange juice. She was from the provincial town of Udon, and studied Chinese. Nothing about her revealed her methods of procuring supplemental income.

There are 200,000 girls working in Thailand at this twilight game, though nothing close to the two million that NGOs once claimed. The majority are freelancers, or parttimers, slippery single-woman entrepreneurs who wheel and deal by themselves, barely noticed by the society around them. Many are migrants from the north, from places like the rice-growing plains of Issan, though Porntip was not one of those. She seemed familiar with the layout of the Primrose Apartments, and with the mental states of the men she did business with. She seemed amused by them. Big, simple children with a twist of guilt inside them. She once told me she could not believe how polite and apologetic they were. Did they think they were doing something wrong? If they did, what was it?

She stayed all afternoon, and afterward we listened to CDs or played Scrabble. There seemed to be no schedule boxing her in, her time was malleable and extendable. When she left I had to pass the banknotes into her hand, a gesture which I had never made before—the damp notes sliding from palm to palm, suddenly weighty and acrimonious, and she caught my eye as if to say "See?" The internal barrier broken.

There is a word in Thai, *sanuk*, which embodies the idea of enjoying life to the full as a duty. It is usually translated as "fun" or "pleasure," but it is really untranslatable. Porntip was a bearer of *sanuk*. She came every fourth day for a month, with a curious punctuality, as if she was coming upriver between classes. Sometimes she said she was avoiding Dennis and made me promise not to tell him. We made love on the wood floor, burning knees and elbows, crushed flat against the white paint of the walls. Once she made me cut off her ponytail with a pair of scissors and laughed for ten minutes. Other times, she was silent, concentrated, determined on something undisclosed. We are told ceaselessly that sex and love are two different things that merge only within monogamy, a tirade straight out of the Dark Ages. It is categorically untrue. With a quick, mysterious tropism one loves every woman one fucks. I loved Porntip, but it didn't have to be elaborated. Even the most disgusting misogynist sex tourist is secretly in love with the thing he tries so hard to defile. That love gnaws at him and you can see it in his furious, ruddy face. And Porntip was only doing this for a year, she said, before she graduated and moved on. She said once:

"This part of the river is haunted. Have you ever heard of Si Ouey? He's buried right next door, in Thonburi. Rapist and murderer! He's in the hospital museum; you should go see him and say hello. Of course I'm not going with you! His ghost is still there. It's still walking about at night. You should be careful."

•

I go a single stop upriver to the Thonburi pier. It is so close
to Wang Lang you can practically see it from the Primrose,
but like Wang Lang very few foreigners stop there and there
is a desultory, shabby quality to the place. Thonburi, on the
left bank of the river, is where Bangkok began. This is where
the early fort was built and where the court resided.

I get off at the pier. It is a scrum of dogs and young soldiers prone on the benches which line the passageway to the
street, a smell of burned grass. There is a large Victorian-
style railway station here, where train operations have been
suspended. A street leads up to Wat Suwannaram, where
Thai royalty used to be cremated. Then there's a sign for the
Siriaj Hospital. The Forensics and Parasitology Museums
can be found on the second floor of the Anatomy Building
in this nondescript hospital founded by King Rama V and
named after his dead baby son.

In the Forensics Museum there are countless photographs of crime and accident scenes with terse captions:
"Multiple Cuts by Propeller," decapitations from train acci-
dents, "Cut Throat by Beer Bottle," cases of crania punc-
tured by gunshots, yellowed mandibles and bottles filled
with damaged brains. On a lighter note, there are the medical gowns worn by the men who investigated the mysterious
murder of the young King Rama VIII in 1946.

Then there are the preserved corpses of serial killers,
which are placed in glass cases with metal basins to catch
their cadaverine wax. In the middle of the room, there's the
shrunken body of the child murderer Si Ouey, sometimes
written in English as Zee-Oui: a Chinese immigrant called Li
Hui who went on a spree of infanticide in the 1950s, eating

the internal organs of the small children he abducted and killed. He is standing, gesticulating, his mouth wide open.

It is like Madame Tussaud's, except that the waxwork is real. And the Forensics Museum is popular with Chinese tourists. It's as if word of mouth has gotten back to China about this unsavory compatriot of theirs, this shameful splinter of the race. They are also curious about the method of his execution: in Thailand the condemned man is shot with a weapon fixed in place, the bullet directed through a square cut into a length of silk. A flower is placed between his tied hands. A single shot through the heart.

When I thought Dennis was lonely, I asked him if he wanted to come along on my night walks, and he eagerly accepted. He walked with a cane, and that made our walks agreeably slow, but never disjointed. It was an opportunity to discuss past lives, past loves. Dennis, unlike McGinnis, was wary and prickly, a man who scanned your sentences as if he was reading them on a moving ticker tape, like financial data. Perhaps it was a skill he had acquired through interviewing thousands of people for mortgages. He would stop you in mid-sentence and make you repeat the first half slowly until he understood it perfectly. His eyes locked into yours and he always smiled, as if what you had to say was so daft that you might as well hang yourself from your own gibbet. It was irritating, but Dennis also had wonderful one-liners.

"Life would be perfectly agreeable," he would say, "if it weren't for all the amusements one has to go through."

We made finds: by the Oriental, through an alley which is partially covered by a Venetian bridge, stands the Catholic cathedral of Bangkok, in an oblong square of French-style trees. There is a white-light sign that says "Catholic Center." I seek out those places that remind me of nocturnal aquaria, where the laws of physics seem to be distorted. A short way down Charung Krung, I found an enclave near the CAT Telecom building—whose tower rises to an unnecessary height—where there was a concentration of shacks and houses, and a temple colored like dried blood. Among these shacks, and from amid a whirl of laundry lines, there rose a beautiful white stupa which seemed to have been completely forgotten by the inhabitants, rising nevertheless into a state of grace.

Some nights we went late to the Shangri-La Hotel by the river. The salons of this opulently tasteless hotel were restful at night because there was no one there but the night cleaners with their vacuums and dusters. A sea of armchairs and sofas, courtly frescoes and chandeliers. Great staircases and marble lobbies leading nowhere. We sat by the windows and watched the river, and Dennis smoked a pipe. It felt like the *Titanic* about to sink, or some other ocean liner of times past whose passengers have abandoned it, and I remember thinking that my grandfather, a trombonist with the Halle Orchestra under Toscanini in the thirties, would have loved this place, and would doubtless have stayed here had he ever come to Bangkok. The Chinese vases shone in the bitter lamplight with a sheen of large insects.

"You're a stiff fella," said Dennis in a friendly way. "I mean, you're a little awkward here, aren't you? Do you know what the maids at the condo call you? Miss Lalant. It's not on purpose. They don't understand the difference between 'Miss' and 'Mister.' And that's how they pronounce your name. Miss Lalant."

His hand shook on the polished knob of his cane. He regarded me with pity, because I must have seemed like all new arrivals, a person wrapped in occidental pieties and superstitions, and for us those pieties are about the self, especially the sexual self. "Look at those men vacuuming the carpets," he said. "I love the way they are neither happy nor unhappy. I wonder if we could be the same."

How would one do it? The Taoists pointed out two thousand years ago that the Good Life consists of perfecting to the greatest possible degree the virtues we share with animals. Not in mastering or subduing them, but in realizing our similarities with them. To gravitate closer to dogs and pachyderms, to monkeys and caterpillars. In Thai Buddhism, the principle of loving-kindness, or *metta*, is embodied by the gecko. The term "animal" shouldn't be an insult, because it points to what is best in humans.

On occasion we took a boat across to Phra Arthit in Rattanakosin. Next to the white Phra Sumain fort, overlooking the river, there's a bandstand and a sprawl of tired gardens. A bridge across the Klong Banglampu connects to an enclave of narrow lanes, above which pots of basil rattle in winds coming off the river. The place is often full of monks. Neither happy nor unhappy: it was an unusual desideratum. I was beginning to see that it certainly applied to Dennis himself, who was interested in "the East," and who liked Bangkok because she was partly Hindu, a piece of India.

"Are you really neither happy nor unhappy?" I asked.

"I like to paint and to make love to Porntit. I am thankful that you can buy generic Viagra without a prescription at any Thai pharmacy. It works out to two dollars a hit. It's pleasure, not happiness, but I am happy with that—if you see what I mean. My wife, God bless her, would never have understood."

Life after life. Is that what this was?

I tried to imagine Mrs. Dennis. They used to go to Polynesia together on holiday. I thought sometimes he was in mourning.

"Maybe," I offered, "she would have understood."

"You didn't know Mavis. A real Anglo-Saxon."

Just like my mother, I thought. Just like me. Do we head to places which we know will undo us, take the long hand of our clock and bend it backward?

•

This part of Rattanakosin just north of the canal which empties into the river is one of the few remnants of the old city that the authorities, no doubt in a fit of absentminded-ness, have neglected to bulldoze. The surfaces of the houses are a vertical maze of cracks and puzzles, in which cicadas are lodged as if they have mistaken it for a man-made forest. It makes you wonder what these now monstrous Asian cities were like before the West became their model of develop-ment. Before the architecture of Citibank became their ideal. Old photographs of Bangkok show wide avenues, lines of trees, a spacious and thoughtful urban planning. The build-ings are set back from the roads and are dignified by façades to which attention has been paid. There were canals every-where, the *klong*. Then, sometime in the nineteenth cen-tury, the Chinese began building densely packed commercial neighborhoods like those of China. The spaces filled in. And finally, between 1960 and 1990, the whole thing was ruth-lessly destroyed. The canals were turned into expressways. The great street of Sathorn was a canal until the 1980s. Migrating birds still massed around its trees as if remember-ing that it was once a body of water. So now it is birds who remember our past more longingly than humans.

But at night at least the bottom layers of this palimpsest could be felt again. The daytime city fell away and the past seeped back up to the surface. Dennis knew all about this sort of thing. It fed his sense of rage that the world, far from improving, was in fact getting worse by the year.

Did I know that the World Meteorological Organization had named Bangkok on average as the hottest large city on earth? Then why, he protested, create a labyrinth of huddled cheap cement, steel, and glass, a living hell? The worst possible arrangement for a city where the average temperature is forty degrees centigrade. "This neighborhood, on the other hand," he said, wobbling on his cane. "There is something tender about it."

Strings of shells moved. This street was like a glass ship that's been shaken. Hundreds of flowerpots emerged from circles of lamplight. Yellow houses with red doors, slanted gardens. A flowering tree spreading right across the street, and an ancient sound of radios. I was glad I had brought Dennis here, because it made him light up. He waxed angry and it made him bright, because every man from a cold race has inside him a well of unspent lava boiling with bitterness and poetry. I thought about my own people: the British officers, the quiet, prudent yeomen, the musty village churches by the river Ouse filled with damp flags and regimental rags. The vicars tabulated back to the time of Oliver Goldsmith. What kind of race were we?

"Everything was for tomorrow," Henry Miller once wrote about his own Nordic ancestors, "but tomorrow never came. The present was only a bridge and on this bridge they are still groaning, as the world groans, and not one idiot thinks of blowing up the bridge."

•

The name Rattanakosin appears as part of Bangkok's original ceremonial name in Thai, which is listed in the Guinness Book of Records as the world's longest place-name: Krungthep Mahanakhon Amonrattanakosin Mahintharayut-

thaya Mahadilokphop Noppharatratchathani Buriromudom-
ratchaniwet Mahasathan Amonphiman Awatansathit Sak-
kathattiya Witsanu Kamprasit.

It is mostly a Thai pronunciation of a blend of Sanskrit
and Pali, the ancient languages of India, and it means: "The
city of angels, the great city, the eternal jewel city, the im-
pregnable city of God Indra, the grand capital of the world
endowed with nine precious gems, the happy city, abound-
ing in an enormous Royal Palace that resembles the heavenly
abode where reigns the reincarnated god, a city given by
Indra and built by Vishnu."

So Bangkok was built by Vishnu.

In the Puranas, Vishnu is described as being dark blue,
the "color of clouds." His four arms hold a mace, a conch, a
scepter, and a chakra. In the Bhagavad Gita, he is glimpsed
by Arjuna and Krishna, to whom he takes the form of blinding galaxies wheeling through infinite time, arcs of cosmic
radiation. The creator and destroyer of all existences.

·

The Thai kings are incarnations of Vishnu. This means that
they are virtual gods, that they partake of the mystery of
godhead. From the Khmer royalty the Thais derived this
idea of *devaraja*, divine kingship, and the enormity of this
fact escapes the majority of visitors. If the society is presided
over by an incarnation of Vishnu, then the whole society
must be permeated by magic. Since the military coup of
1932, the Thai kings have not been absolute monarchs. But
they are far more powerful than British, Swedish, or Dutch
monarchs. They are more potent than the similarly godlike
Japanese emperor. The title they take, that of Lord Rama,

reveals their lofty status in the cosmic hierarchy. There were nine Ramas between 1782 and 2007; the present king, Bumiphol, is Rama IX. Nine kings, just as there are supposed to be nine incarnations of Vishnu. It is the most mystical monarchy in existence. The Chakri dynasty that founded Bangkok is synonymous with the city.

It is also a Theravada monarchy. Buddhism is divided into two main branches. The earlier, purer, form was known in India as Hinayana, or "the little raft" (in Sanskrit). Based closely on the early Buddhist scriptures known as the Pali Canon, it adhered to the Buddha's original conception of a political state based on his teaching. It spread early on to Sri Lanka and Burma. It began to call itself Theravada—"the way of the elders"—perhaps to avoid sounding minoritarian.

The other branch, known as Mahayana, "the big raft," is the form Buddhism took as it spread to societies with complex political traditions of their own, such as Tibet, China, and Japan. These societies did not want Buddhists telling them how to organize their states. Instead, they took the metaphysical dimensions of the religion and fused it with their own colorful mythologies, creating what Theravada purists saw as a corrupted, hybrid Buddhism. But Mahayana is the dominant Buddhism of Asia.

Living here, one becomes increasingly aware of the nine Buddhist kings who are also incarnations of Vishnu, these Ramas who are called *Phranam* in Thai. There are even nine expressways, named after each. It is Rama IV and V, though, who most dominate the popular imagination. They ruled during the uncertain period when the Kingdom of Siam was encountering the West for the first time, the second half of the nineteenth century. The British and French were all around them, in Malaya, in Indochina, in Burma, in India.

But Thailand remained the only society to never be colonized by a European power. Rama IV, also known as Mongkut, was the overbearing semi-archaic monarch in *The King and I*, and the subject of a dubious memoir by the English governess Anna Leonowens, who taught his children in the early 1860s. The 1956 film with Yul Brynner is considered so offensive to Thais that it is still banned in Thailand. They say it insults the divine kingship.

•

But the relations between the impetuous, barking king, torn between East and West, and the indomitable, slightly uptight Englishwoman gave such life to the Rodgers and Hammerstein musical, and then the film, because it could be read as a struggle between Asia and Europe. During his life, Yul Brynner played Rama IV over four thousand times onstage, and of course in the film. Anna herself wrote a sensationalist book in which she claimed to have witnessed the public burning of a slave called Tuptim, and to have seen underground dungeons beneath the Royal Palace. The Thais said she was a born fabricator.

Her student was Prince Chulalongkorn, who became Rama V in 1868. Fluent in English, a European gentleman, dapper and slim, the abolisher of slavery in Thailand, Rama the Great ruled until 1910 and took the kingdom into its own quirky version of modernity. In the hand-colored photographs he looks like a large elf with his polished mustache and lace-up shoes, a top hat poised on his knee, his assurance subtly muted.

There is a tormented drama between these three remarkable characters. Was Chulalongkorn a product of Ms.
Leonowens and her English ways? The intelligent, cunning
Mongkut was not as archaic as he is portrayed, and his
spurning of the brittle English governess went hand in hand
with a desire that his son be open to the idea of telescopes
and steam engines.

Anna's story, however, was eventually unraveled by the
entomologist A. S. Bristowe, an expert in Asian spiders, who
showed without much difficulty that most of it was indeed
invented, as the Thais always asserted.

•

Anna claims she was born Anna Henriette Crawford in
Caernarfon, Wales, in 1834, the daughter of a British Army
captain named Thomas Crawford. Bristowe, however, that
indefatigable tracer of the ancestry of spiders, found no
record of any such birth. Instead, he discovered that she was
born in 1831 in India, to a cabinetmaker turned army ser-
geant by the name of Thomas Edwards and a half-Indian
woman named Mary Anne Glasscott. In 1845, her elder sister, Eliza, married a British civil servant named Edward
John Pratt—their grandson, William Henry Pratt, metamor-
phosed into the movie star Boris Karloff, most famous of all
of Frankenstein's monsters.

After her army husband died in 1859, leaving his widow
and children in dire straits, Anna opened a school for officers' children in Singapore. The Siamese consulate, hearing
of this school, offered her a post at the court of King
Mongkut, teaching English. The move into an unconquered,
un-Europeanized world must have been shocking. Mongkut

had thirty-nine wives and eighty-nine children. He was, after
all, an incarnation of Vishnu.

For five years, she lived close to the court, and close to
the Crown Prince (when they met thirty years later in London, in 1897, he expressed his debt to her). She became a
friend of Harriet Beecher Stowe and made *Uncle Tom's
Cabin* a known book in royal circles, where the antislavery
message might have displeased Mongkut, but not his son.

After Rama IV's death, Anna went to Nova Scotia,
where she founded the Novia Scotia College of Art and
Design and emerged as a noted feminist and suffragette. She
died in Montreal in 1915, at the age of eighty-one.

Bristowe began by researching the life of Anna's son,
Louis, who stayed in Siam, became an officer in the Royal
Siamese Cavalry, and founded a Bangkok trading company
which still bears his name. Bristowe set out to look behind
the novelization of Anna's memoirs (originally published
serially in *The Atlantic Monthly*) by the writer Margaret
Landon in 1944.

And so it is all lies. Anna is the first *farang* to use
Siam/Thailand as a place to reinvent herself, to turn herself
into a "character." You could do this only in a place that
was not yet a colony. In a non-colony there would be no
infrastructure of verification, such that nobody could check
you up. It's possible, though, that Anna's memoir is a kind
of political argument, where inventions and exaggerations
serve some purpose. They are a scaffold upon which emotions are hung.

As a memoir, it doesn't try to relate facts, but then memoirs are rarely empirical in nature. They are statements of
purpose, descriptions of life as the writer *would like it to be*.

Many will find this unacceptable, but the faultless memoir doesn't exist—indeed, it's a lame, moralistic fantasy. Every memoir can be fact-checked and proved wrong. But Bristowe's unraveling of Anna's family history doesn't prove that she didn't see an execution.

The memoir is a treacherous form. Chateaubriand described a 1791 visit to Niagara Falls in his *Mémoires d'outre-tombe*, and for centuries Frenchmen visiting Niagara Falls took their Chateaubriand with them, extolling the power and veracity of his description of them. Only recently has it been suggested that Chateaubriand may have never gone anywhere near Niagara Falls. Doubters allege that he cobbled his marvelous description of them from various sources. The greatest memoir ever written, the model of the genre—and at its center a plagiarism, a collage, a sleight of hand. If Chateaubriand were alive today he would be flayed on *Oprah*, disgraced, banished. Where, it would be asked, were the fact-checkers? But do those who read Chateaubriand stop reading *Mémoires d'outre-tombe*?

It began to occur to me that Thailand as a place of exile sometimes fosters a taste for self-invention which is not unrelated to her cosmology. Where the Blue God reigns, you could say, all is magical and relative. For who is Vishnu exactly, and how can a king incarnate something so vast? Memoirs seem petty commercial affairs when put next to the wheeling galaxies that make up Vishnu's cosmic body. The Blue God, too, takes on multiple disguises, changes form like supercharged putty. In the scenes with Arjuna in the Bhagavad Gita, he is at one moment the sweet and handsome charioteer Krishna, at the next the nearest thing in literature to a vision of nuclear holocaust. "I am become Death," he says mildly, "the destroyer of worlds." He encourages a view of reality that is undependable, plastic, ever-shifting, myste-rious. He needs no fact-checkers.

W. S. Bristowe's *Louis and the King of Siam* (1976), meanwhile, is an engaging read, and in its unswerving dedi-cation to scientific fact it is almost on a par with his critical work of 1939, *The Comity of Spiders*.

By the naval dockyards the winter heat was not yet oppressive, the streets still had a brisk cleanliness which they lose in the rainy season. Trok Matoom is opposite the naval dockyards, and I came here to eat bael fruit boiled in syrup. There are alleys in Bangkok—sometimes called *trok*—where a single foodstuff is made. A single boiled fruit in this case, for which the whole alley is named—bael is *matoom*. There is another alley nearby called Trok Khao Mao, which produces shredded rice mixed with rain-tree leaves.

It is like medieval London, specific products and services concentrated in a single street. Bael in hand, I wandered from Wang Lang pier down Amarin Boulevard to the Mon canal, wincing in the traffic, the syrup dripping over my fingers, walking all the way back to the intersection with Phran Nok.

I made this walk every day, because it was at hand, easy to do, and because I could do it without getting lost, without fumbling for maps. I paused on the bridge over the Mon canal, where the Mon people were once gatekeepers, and wondered at the moldering sluice gates and hydraulic apparatus, covered with potted plants, which never seemed to be put to work: the inertia of all that machinery seemed so symptomatic of a city that stirred itself to efficiency only when it felt like it. The Wat Khreuwan temple bordering the canal sends a slender white cremation chimney into

the water's reflections, and sometimes it puffs with cremated ash.

Here, in Bangkok Yai, the dying city lies in its bed, like
an old man on his side smoking a pipe. Amarin means
"angel" in Thai, and this boulevard of angels is wide, raffish, laid-back, at least at night. Rare for Bangkok, one can
walk without too much physical effort, stopping under the
trees. You pass the same things every night. The hole in the
wall filled with waving girls (no sign, no light, just the girls);
Wang Doem, the side street that arches down to Wat Arun,
lined with cream-colored wooden houses with carefully
painted shutters. From Wang Doem, little *sois* named after
the temple run across the Ban Mo canal; children's play-
grounds sit underneath the overpasses. There are plants
everywhere. Through cracks in the corrugated iron you see
old ladies in metal chairs watching soaps on tiny black-and-
white televisions.

If I had not discovered the world of Amarin, I would
never have stayed in Bangkok. There are places that are
incapable of prettifying their pasts for an ulterior motive,
that cannot preserve anything consciously. In Paris, with all
its immaculate restorations, I would feel guilty and exposed:
not perfect enough. In Bangkok, one can decay freely.

Night after night I mapped out the meanderings of the
little-known Ban Mo canal that pops up all along Amarin,
weaving its own way through canal slums, spanned by
cement girders. As Wang Doem curves around the naval
base next to Wat Arun, it passes the Ban Mo again, and here
there are gardens ten feet square perched precariously over
her water and assembled by old couples with nothing better
to do.

Gradually, however, I pushed farther on, toward the Yai canal and its larger bridge. On the far side of this bridge you come to the Patthanakison Music School and Museum, which sits by the road, announced by a humble sign: an incision between the slum houses leads you there. This tunnel leads to the walls of the school, and then to Wat Kalayanimit; you can walk all around its circumference until you are suddenly wandering down avenues of weeds between the buildings, past weathered, bell-shaped *chedi*s. The place is half ruined, though it was built by Rama III in the early nineteenth century. Its blackened, elegant spires are surrounded these days by wooden scaffolds which sustain an army of restorers. Slowly, the antique ceramics are coming back to life and Kalayanimit's headless sculptures might one day re-acquire their missing appendages. You are close to the river again, and the candy-pink tower of the old Portuguese Santa Cruz Church. At night these river temples are filled with dogs that follow you at a distance like wolf packs, and at the temple's pier there are slippery men who ask you where you are going. Suddenly you are back to the glare of the present century.

On the river stands the exquisite Chinese temple of Kuan an Keng, set back from the water by a stone courtyard shaded by trees, its surfaces covered with decayed frescoes of storks and cranes etched in delicate blues and blacks and ruined, as a notice tells us, "by rain and bats." Some of the frescoes are three-dimensional, with scenes of merchant street life; finely sculpted little robed bodies lean out of the walls, most of them decapitated, or the faces carefully gouged out, as if those heads had once depicted real people and therefore possessed talismanic value which made them

worth stealing or defacing. They are the last traces of the
Hokkien merchants who built the temple 170 years ago. But
the Simasathien family, who now own and maintain the
Keng, have not restored them, and this is better in a way: the
temple has a wounded beauty which would be lost with
improvements.

Behind it, the atmosphere of merry ruin continues along
Soi Kudejeen 7. Houses and their yards overflowing with
wildflowers, piles of marine debris, waves crashing under the
houses, spirit houses in whorls of trash. And people living
here, seemingly unconcerned, lithe and slightly furtive like
crabs clinging to rocks that will eventually be atomized.

•

If a city is divided into night and day, as Bangkok is, you
should stick to night. I noticed that my feet were changing
shape as I walked for miles in open sandals, acclimatizing to
tropical labors, and that my cock, my Roger the Dodger,
was responding not to the presence of thousands of street-
walkers (since here there were none) but to the alien quality
of a cuisine which the insipid Thai restaurants of home had
not prepared me for.

I turned onto Phran Nok. The end of day, the best time
of the twenty-four-hour cycle, the lush, quivering beginning
of night. The hour of smoke from woks. I wanted strange
foods. Not just gold-skinned eggs and oolong tea, and banana leaves, but things that would break me open, take me
to the further side of a taboo.

At the corner of Phran Nok, in the first minutes of night,
I noticed the mobile restaurants which are such a feature of
the metropolis, small motorbikes fitted out with trays lit

from above by bare lightbulbs. Sometimes they whiz by you at high speed, a snack bar on two wheels, mounds of boiled shrimp and wontons. The operators are little old men with tattoos, the genies of night food. On the market street that leads down to the river, where a riot of cheap clothing competes with thousands of pale-green lottery tickets, they would arrive with their wares all lit up with waxy yellow light. *Farang*s rarely approach them, either because you have to speak Thai or because anything you could point at looks like a cautionary tale in the making. The shrimp and wontons are all right; but there are mobile snack bars specializing in insects, a staple food of Thai construction workers. They are like natural history museums on wheels. What they offer requires an entire lexicon—a body of scholarship—to decipher.

Insects are eaten almost everywhere. In Indonesia they even make a snack out of curried dragonflies called "sky prawn." But worms and insects have been canceled, by biblical decree, from the diet of Caucasians.

At Phran Nok I waited for the bikes to stop. It is like approaching a hooker for the first time. The old men are insect pimps. They look you steadily in the eye as you come up, then remove an aerosol from under the contraption. It is filled with "special sauce." You peruse the wares as the Thais look on, and you realize that the trays are mostly filled with giant waterbugs and fried worms called *rot duan*, or "express trains." These worms feed on bamboo and have a slightly sweet, peanuty taste. But there are also silkworm cocoons, grasshoppers, and cicadas fried in coconut oil. The vendor takes a pink paper napkin (they are indigenous to the country) and wraps a giant water beetle, *Cybister tripunc-*

tatus. He holds it out like an ice-cream cone. He then approaches with the aerosol and gives it a burst of special sauce.

Your first waterbug: what a relief. It isn't really necessary, it's just that one doesn't want to be a *square* to oneself. And food is what changes our perspective on things without the mind even being involved. Bite into a waterbug and all exoticism is shattered.

•

My initiation into *maeng-da*—insects—was the first step in a disengagement from the habits of a lifetime, the system of taste that holds a human being together from childhood on, though it didn't mean that from then on I would be eating "express trains" every afternoon after my walk along Thanon Amun Arun Amarin. It was just that the *Cybister tripunctatus* nativized me physically. Eating it disrupted the normal flow of reactions and then made my solitary walks more loose, more improvisational. Some weeks I went searching for a single thing, like the pink soup made from fermented tofu and preserved squid called *yen ta foh*, or else the so-called sour ants.

Sour ants, their eggs like packets of pus that burst on the back of the tongue. Farlo, living as he did in rural Cambodia half the year, was an especially able amateur of such things. He knew where to find a country specialty like red ant soup in the city, and I had the impression that when times were hard and tourists nowhere to be found in the bars of Battambang, he and his young Khmer wife lived on ant soup for days on end. Because he seemed to be a connoisseur of moveable feasts, I sometimes took him with me on the afternoon trek to the naval dockyards, Farlo in his battle fatigues and his military beret, rolling from side to side like an apple in water, his eyes wide and staring and slightly frightened. He was in Bangkok to recruit tourists for his lodge, and employed ingenious methods to do this. Not only did he charm all the travel agents along the tourist axes with his tales of life in the pristine Cardamom Mountains, but he went to hotel bars and struck up conservations with random strangers who looked as if they might be suitable material for Paradise Lodge. It netted him about twelve tourists a year, barely enough to live on but sufficient to stave off outright starvation. His wife and baby awaited him back in Samlok.

We walked all over the districts called Taling Chan, Bang Philat, and the larger area of Bangkok Noi, which contains Wang Lang. We followed Amarin down to the Mon canal, eating all the way like grazing wildebeest, with sticky hands that couldn't be cleaned.

"It's fine being lost, isn't it?" said the British soldier who always knew where he was (and if he didn't, he took out a military compass).

The Nang Kwak dolls in all the shops—the Beckoning Lady—with a hand raised to draw you in, and the feline equivalent, the Japanese *maneki-neko* with its similarly raised right paw; the Indian tailors with their black-clothed dummies equipped with startling white eyes, the tailor himself peering through the window with a turban glittering with pins; the miles of terse metal shutters, the high curbs of broken stones colored like laterite, the men sewing outside on ancient Flying Man machines, pedaling furiously, and the high-tech coffee shops bathed in toothpaste-blue neon which

are always stacked with magazines and mysterious instruc-
tional booklets written in Thai but with English titles like
Sex Code for You.

•

When we stopped for tea, Farlo told me all about the war in
Angola. It sounded fantastical, Homeric. Had such things
happened such a short time ago? For some men, war was a
moveable feast as well.

"The war in Rhodesia was even worse. All that suffering
for nothing. After that, there was nae going back to England
for me. I had a piece of shrapnel in me head."

"How did the shrapnel turn you into an exile?"

"I was already exiled. The military life is exile. Have you
seen how many servicemen there are in Bangkok? We're a
whole tribe, a whole lost tribe."

He had a former wife back in England, two grown-up
sons. What could they make of his living in a self-made
lodge in the Cardamom Mountains, making conservation
efforts on behalf of the rare Cardamom tiger, having neigh-
borly tea times with the old Khmer Rouge leaders?

"They're just glad I'm no longer an alcoholic."

His hand shook, just like Dennis's. It seemed that so
many expats' hands shook here. A hospital ward for mentally shattered people . . .

"I have dreams about roads in Angola almost every
night. Just roads. Roads where things happened. An artillery
barrage. An ambush. I was never afraid then. But now it's a
different matter."

It was difficult to know how much of what he said was
true—not the statements themselves, but the motives behind

them. The British make up the largest contingent of foreign visitors to Thailand, and probably the largest contingent of *farang* permanent residents. I wouldn't be surprised (Lawrence Durrell: "English life is really like an autopsy"). Farlo was always pestering me to come and visit him in Samlok, as if to verify that he had made a success of his life. But the restless drive which had turned him into a mercenary in the first place hadn't been assuaged. He roamed Bangkok like a hungry rat, not knowing quite what he was looking for. Ant soup, *mot som*, a sunset by a bridge, a girl for the night: you couldn't pin down what he wanted. Westerners choose Bangkok as a place to live precisely because they can never understand it, for even the Thai script, that variation of written Sanskrit, is impossible to master. It's this ignorance which comforts the *farang*. However conversant in Thai culture, he will never get close to the bottom of it.

One night Farlo took me out dancing to a club in Silom, and after a few hours he was there on the dance floor by himself, spinning around like a middle-aged top, arms akimbo, high on Ecstasy, his grizzled white stubble shining like frost in a strobe light. It is like Cavafy's Alexandria, which always seems suffocating—

> *You tell yourself: I'll be gone*
> *To some other land, some other sea.*
> *To a city lovelier far than this*
> *Could ever have been or hoped to be—*
> *Where every step now tightens the noose . . .*

The rains began, and around the Primrose puddles opened up. The maid waddled through them with guttural sighs, muttering the word *hoi*, a word from the slums which imitates the snort of an irritated water buffalo. "You're telling me!" You could hear drops hitting the seething river. In pockets, the city has a surprising quietness, an absolute tranquillity. Heat steams the window glass, and through it the banana leaves dip down under the onslaught, with a swaying rhythm. And yet it's not the rainy reason, just a premature taste of it.

•

McGinnis knocked on the door. He wanted to play chess on the balcony and he had a water pipe with him, one of those tin models they sell for a few baht in Little Arabia on Sukhumvit Soi 3.

"It's raining cats and dogs," he argued. "You can't possibly work when it's raining animals."

He was in pajamas with Thai sandals, a paper hat on his head made out of the *Bangkok Post*. We set up a table, arranging the pipe, the coffee, French pastries from Black Canyon, plum jam, spring rolls. He paid for everything because I was down to 500 baht and it had to last.

"I'm getting a check," I said.

"Oh, you're getting a check?"

He glanced at the kitchen, where there was nothing except an occasional cockroach scurrying across the walls.

"I hear," he said, leaning forward, "that the other Britisher, Farlo, *eats insects.*"

"It's impossible."

"He eats *maeng-da*. I guess he went savage out there in Cambodia."

McGinnis had those merry eyes that always shake one to the core. As I tore through the pastries, he asked, "Did you eat yesterday?"

"I'm on a budget. The thing about insects is that they're cheap. A whole cup of 'express trains' for a handful of baht. What a bargain."

He went on: "It's a shame you're so broke. We could go slumming if you had a bit of cash. I could advance you, though."

"I don't pay for girls," I said coldly.

"Ah, I think you do, my friend. We are all jolly with Porntip from time to time. No need to blush, you look like an idiot. It's not clear in any man's mind, whatever he pretends, though of course I exclude the prigs, who are about half the male population. The Noble Ones, I call them. Too noble for us, eh? Yes, we're all fairly noble. Except when it comes to sleaze. I *love* sleaze. I do hate those people who give you a canty shudder when they utter the word 'sleaze.' As if they are so superior to it that it's unthinkable that it would even cross their minds. Except when they're asleep, of course. You know, those Salem women and those Germanic men in sandals with their rolling eyes. I mean, Christ, you'd think they'd have *some* imagination when it comes to our regrettable sex. I call them the Aphids. A man who has no taste whatsoever for sleaze is half dead, or maybe even totally dead, because he is tormented by the Aphids. Whereas *we* prefer at least to be tormented by our *genuine* demons. All we need is another word to replace 'whore,' 'hooker,' 'prostitute.' "

"In the States, they call them providers."

"Lovely. Actually I like it, very warm and cozy. But no. There's no glamour in that. Still, it's accurate enough."

He looked at me coolly, and I noticed for the first time that he had blue eyes with little fragments of goat around them. I suddenly didn't believe that he was from Newhaven at all. A gypsy of the highest order, a minor rake. But a rake who has thought out all his options with a dry eye. As if at a certain point he had asked himself how he was going to age, to decline, and what manner of disgrace he was going to opt for. What was the alternative?

He tapped the table. "You're looking over your shoulder. You're looking over your shoulder and what do you see?"

"I'm not looking over my shoulder."

"A beautiful blond girlfriend with reproaching blue eyes. Don't look over your shoulder. That lovely girlfriend is busy fucking someone else as we speak. Someone nicer, someone richer. Someone tamer. Someone who does what he's told."

Since this was altogether certain, I said nothing.

"I find it surprising that you say you don't pay for it. Whereas in fact your professional standing, your earning power, is constantly being assessed by women. They never marry beneath themselves. Have you not noticed that?"

"It was my choice to come here."

"Well, there you are, then." He opened up a glassy

smile. "When in Rome do as the Romans." But what did the Romans do?

"I've been to Rome, too," he laughed. "Awful place to get laid."

In fact, you couldn't understand Bangkok without considering the difficulty of procuring even the most facile pleasures in Europe and America, and he supposed one would have to add Japan.

Take Italians. That was a nice relaxed country, wasn't it? No it wasn't. It was a dreary, repressed sexual police state. Thailand, he went on, was filled with Italian men trying to get laid. The clubs were packed with them. Thai cities teemed with Italians because when all was said and done the land of *amore* apparently didn't satisfy them very much. They were frustrated half to death, and a good percentage of the neon signs in Pattaya said things like *Camera Libera* and *Pizzeria Bienvenuti*. Which proved that the Thais at least read them correctly, as they read all *farang*s correctly.

"It's not a very salubrious picture. I can stomach a sex-starved Brit, but an Italian?"

McGinnis was a devious chess player, with hands that shot across the board like crows pecking at meat. He played rapidly, without making mistakes, and his eyes did not move. There was a precarity in his look at all times, something hanging by its fingernails from a cliff. It made you want to tread on those hands to loosen their grip, to see the Englishman in his polka-dot cravat spiral downward toward a distant dried riverbed, fluttering in the wind, turning like a doomed kite until he hit the stones and shattered into rags. It was those dulled, irregular teeth.

"I am not that poor."

"Oh, come off it. You don't have a pot to piss in."

"It's a lovely expression, isn't it?"

"We are in the East, comrade, and here we must think in the Eastern way. Not the fuckers and swamis and the Beatles. No, I mean seriously."

"I hate it when people talk about the wisdom of the East. Really, McGinnis, I go to sleep."

"Yes, yes. But have you considered Krishna's arrow?"

•

I looked across the river. I had 476 baht to last me five days and I no longer wanted to know what that came to in dollars. A single sandwich in Manhattan. A toilet roll in Tokyo. A Thai electricity bill.

"Anyway," he snapped, "is money so very simple? Then why don't you have any? Never mind. I could give you an advance, you know." His eyes brightened. "We could go to the Eden Club!"

The Eden Club was a "two girl" club on Soi 7/1 on Sukhumvit, and it specialized in role-playing sessions, with hundreds of in-house costumes to cater to every whim. Its main room, McGinnis explained, had a yellow line running down its center, with the women separated into two sections. What did it mean? It was a mystery that had to be solved by the client himself. The owner was a Frenchman who gave you a laminated menu of services. Every session had to be booked with two girls, never one. Two girls, the clients would say afterward. You haven't lived till you've had two girls dressed up as Asian nuns.

"I don't have that fantasy," I said. "I don't have the nun-despoiling fantasy."

"I'm just giving you nuns as an example. You can dress them as vicars if you want. Two Asian vicars. Think about that, two corrupt vicars in high heels."

"I don't want vicars, either."

"I've heard that Dennis dresses them up as sanitation workers. I like New York cops myself. I have an arrest complex. They have real leather holsters, too." If I wouldn't do vicars, he said, there was something else I could do if I insisted on being so broke. Broke men went to the hotel bars and allowed themselves to be fished up by a class of middle-aged Japanese women who flew over from Tokyo for precisely this purpose. It was quite a trade. At the Peninsula, for example, all one had to do was sit at the bar and make eyes at the middle-aged Japanese women there.

"What about Krishna's arrow?" I asked.

McGinnis stirred slightly. He had it all prepared in his mind. "It's that scene in the Bhagavad Gita. Krishna is explaining to Arjuna what his attitude to action must be. Arjuna is about to lead his army against the evil Kauravas on the battlefield of Kuru. The Kauravas are the hundred sons of the blind king Dhritarashtra. But they are also Arjuna's cousins, his blood, so to speak. He asks Krishna if it is moral to shoot his bow in anger at them. It is curious, because everyone thinks Hinduism is all about inaction, passivity, renunciation. But not at all. Krishna says, in effect, 'By all means, shoot your bow.' It is in fact moral to act, to be decisive. But it is not moral to attach yourself to the fruit of that action. When you no longer care where the arrow strikes, or if it strikes, you shoot it with unerring determination and accuracy. You become the unattached arrow, liberated from its purpose and effect—but you also become pure

action. I wonder if this idea made its way across the centuries to China, so that Lao-tzu could say, 'The highest man
is at rest as if dead, and in movement he is like a machine.
He knows neither why he is at rest, nor why he is not. Nor
does he know why he is in movement and why he is not.' So
freedom, you see, is like being a machine—or a dog."

At nine, the bar of the Peninsula was half empty. It is a grandiose hotel, rather than a grand one, popular with honeymooning couples, Indian millionaires, trade delegations from Singapore and Hong Kong, single *farang* women traveling for business, upper-class riffraff of all races, drinkers on expense accounts, visiting entertainers and celebrities, and lonely aging Japanese women on the prowl for Sí Señora. I sat at the bar, looking shabby and out of place, and parsed how much I would have to spend on a single drink. On the far side of the windows the gardens rolled down to the embankment lit with torches, and the piers where the boats came in. The river looked like a sea. In one corner of the bar a very large black woman sat sprawled and fast asleep, decked out in a startling purple outfit with a matching hat quivering with real flowers. She dripped with heavy gold jewelry, diamond rings, and brooches, and the Thai staff seemed afraid to disturb her.

The hotel bars are where East and West mix their palettes most gaily, on the canvas of sex. There were a number of aging Japanese ladies, heavily made up, dressed in all the right clothes, their eyes hunting for exit doors, and before long one of them made me a sign from the end of the bar, a woman of about fifty, painted red and black like a poisonous insect. She spoke little English and despite her flagrant invitation she was guarded, looking at her mouth frequently in a mirror. There were amazing rings on her hands. She said her name was Ari. Soon we were almost alone in the bar. She looked over at the snoring woman and said, "Arepa Frankin." She said it over and over, seriously, until I understood that this woman was Aretha Franklin. We laughed.

"Of course it isn't," I said.

"Yes," she suddenly said in English. "Yes, it is."

We went upstairs in a mirrored elevator. Halfway up, at around the eighth floor, she took my hand and said something in Japanese. A panic overwhelmed me which she could have seen had she looked. How could I get out of this now, hurtling upward toward our boudoir, hand in hand? We went into a penthouse suite, with unopened packages from stores lying all around it, and I sat on the bed. Ari went to the bathroom and soon I heard taps running, then the shower unit. She had left her handbag on the night table and it was open.

It's at moments like these, exalted and rarified, that one realizes that almost nothing in one's behavior is determined by conscious motives. I lifted my hand and pried into the handbag, knowing there must be money there. It just happened, because it had to, and I felt a moment's guilt, but the taps were running, the suite was overloaded with luxury items, each one worth a month's rent at the Primrose. I pulled out two thousand-baht notes, which felt like they had been extracted from the warm rollers of an ATM only minutes earlier. Then, as I crossed the room, I heard a faint sobbing coming from the bathroom, though perhaps it had been there all along, disguised by the running taps.

It was then that she came out of the bathroom in a flannel hotel robe, her hair wrapped in a towel and her face bloated. I was caught halfway to the door and she roasted me with a look in which there was no awareness of the possibility that I might be leaving, since after all it was *she who picked me up*, and she pulled me back to the bed from where there was no escape. I said I had a headache, but she shook her head. No, no, that would not cut it. She slipped a hand toward me, and found Sí Señora, who works for himself anyway. "Arepa Frankin," she said.

"No, it couldn't be."

I didn't want to touch her, because I had her stolen money in my front pocket, and you can't touch someone whose money you've just stolen. At least I draw the line there.

"You come now," she cried.

Face to face on the bed, kneeling together, clothed, it was a contortion, a ruse. Her hair was freshly washed and dried, for that was what she had been doing in the bathroom.

As a casual sarcasm, I said, "You should pay me," and I waited to see how she would respond. But she said nothing at first. She wrote down her phone number and took the towel from her hair. It had been dyed a deep henna red. She didn't see the joke, and now she wanted to be in control, as if she had paid me. "I will not pay," she insisted. All right, no pay. "No pay, no pay," she cried. Had I misunderstood all along? We continued to "argue," but it was punctuated by laughter which neither of us quite understood. The more she cried about pay, the more I instinctively fumbled for the few remaining banknotes in my pocket. She had a fetish and it was a cute one—it was vaguely connected to doctors and nurses, to childhood games, to my pretending to be a john. I wish women had fetishes more often than they do, though it is probably just that they hide them.

In sex, the comedy of misunderstanding between East and West is what arouses Western men so much. But most fantasies are about strangers, not the people we live with. As tales, they are cruel, detached, anonymous; they revolve around submission, degradation, and symbolic rape. The lover who peddles his fantasies too easily is a fake. Fantasies should probably be kept close to the breast, where they belong, because once idly spoken, they are no longer fantasies at all but exhibitionism. It would take a strong personality to accept your real fantasies if you expressed them clearly.

Intentionally or otherwise, however, the East-West encounter is nearly always redeemed by being slightly comical, but it's not a comedy which has any vicious intent. The Western man is not being mocked, nor is the Eastern woman. It is a difficult waltz to describe, but it could be called a quick, knowing dance of perfectly intentional ignorance. It's a way of making sex innocent again.

Ari. Her look of fixed concentration. I imagine her sitting in the plane from Tokyo to Bangkok, a blank expression on her face as she goes through in her mind all the exercises of desire she is going to get up to at the Peninsula Hotel. I have heard that they go to all the Asian cities now, Hong Kong, Singapore, Kuala Lumpur, looking for Caucasian cock. We are not the only sex tourists. And they are looking for the same thing as their male equivalents: anonymity.

I went down through the gardens to the piers, and crossed to the Oriental in one of the hotel boats. Two thousand baht: I could eat a snack at the Bamboo Bar. Even better, I could avoid the Bamboo Bar altogether and take an eighty-baht cab ride to Sukhumvit Road, where I could eat for twenty-five baht and then walk around—for a change—with some disposable income. It didn't seem like a bad plan, for all its imprecision. But it also struck me, as I sat in the boat, that Ari might call the Peninsula security, and I looked behind me nervously during the crossing. Once on the right bank, I went down the side street alongside the Oriental and got into a taxi. The driver asked me where I wanted to go. We were already speeding down Charung Krung toward the expressway, as if he had decided himself. We came to the corner of Silom, the hospitable glitter of gay bars and the great doomed urban spaces that seem to surround elevated roads and their cement pillars. Blue neon carved out the word *Balls*. Crowds merged at this corner from several directions, like the feelers of giant snails, bombarded by yellow and blue light.

These crowds poured along wide avenues, unhurried, very unlike the crowds of New York, which are always rushing somewhere. Loitering crowds, slow-paced and inquisitive, as is often the case in hot climates. We rushed down Sathorn, however, and the masses thinned out. The avenue

widened, banks and hotels soared up on both sides, and at
the entrances to the various complexes stood those characteristic Thai security guards who are always dressed in
military uniforms, often white with peaked caps, gold
epaulettes, sashes and buttons, and plenty of braid. They
stand with the peaks of their caps just above their eyes,
hands folded, sometimes holding an illuminated stick to
direct traffic. They must think of themselves as the guardians
of ebb and flow, the promoters of organic order. And they
remind you that it is indeed a hierarchical, orderly society,
with Vishnu and the king at the top and rice farmers at the
bottom. In the middle of this sleek boulevard, meanwhile,
the trees seemed stranded, the remnants of orchards long
chopped down, and here and there old buildings flashed
by—an old customs house, I think, looking like a ruin as old
as Angkor, with cornices smoothed by acid rain.

It is uncanny how quickly things age here. Thais believe
that any building that has been inhabited before them is
potentially haunted. Rather than accommodate the possibility of ghosts they tear them down in order to build new,
unhaunted ones. It isn't just capitalism that has modified and
reshaped the old city, therefore—it's also ancient Thai superstition. By the same token, things are built quicker in
Bangkok than anywhere in the world. The skyline changes a
few inches every night. The construction sites are perpetually
active, their arc lamps blazing across the city without a
moment's pause. As we swept into Whittayu, I thought that
even this street had changed since I had seen it a week
earlier. People walked along with transparent umbrellas,
through polluted rain. The buildings shone with gold and
palm green. Showrooms, atriums, lobbies in the wedding-

cake neoclassic style called *satai roman*, a whole language of newly arrived, triumphant affluence. It is all put together like a series of boxes within boxes, intimately organized so that there is not one inch of idle space. Long streets of dense commercial packing, shop after shop, commodities and seductions crammed into what look like ribbons of precious metals and light displays. I got out at Soi 2.

•

I paced up and down the brightly lit stretch of sidewalk between the gas station at Soi Nana 4 and the corner where the Marriott stands behind a strip of postmodern shrubbery. The Chaerung Pharmacy stands here with cats asleep on its counters and ginseng roots suspended in jars of liquid. The punters come here for their generic Viagra hits, Indian "Kanegra" in four-pill blister packs which they carry off to the Nana Entertainment Complex nearby. Next to the pharmacy, a large pub filled with rentable girls and, a little way down, a sign in cheerfully toxic colors: *No-Hands Restaurant*. With 1,850 baht in pocket, I wondered about this. It was Ari's money and I couldn't spend it lackadaisically. The door to the No-Hands place was flanked by two girls in silk tunics, in strange hats. They beckoned with fanciful gestures of four hands. Hands, they seemed to be saying, aren't they beautiful things?

I went up to the doors and they parted slightly, four hands shimmering around me. It looked like a normal restaurant, with circular tables and cushion seating close to the floor.

The restaurant itself was arranged like a saloon. I might have expected elegant Japanese businessmen, but in fact the tables were occupied by Englishmen dressed in the international uniform of Englishmen in the tropics: an Arsenal shirt, camouflage shorts, sneakers, diver watches, and ribbed socks. It's a terrible look, depressing and alarming at the same time. Why do among the wealthiest people in Europe invariably look so shabby, so downtrodden? We know that they do it on purpose, that they are having us on. Are they trying to make everyone miserable? Thais call them "pigeon-shit *farang*s." The Englishman's reputation for dash, you think mournfully, is now two generations dead, and moreover the English always hang together in a herd so that the effect is magnified and you cannot get away from them. They are good-natured to talk to, but don't expect any refinement. They whine and cajole and complain and tell dirty jokes. At best, they are middle-of-the-road, bland, filled with a cowlike resignation. But at the same time their sense of superiority is without dents, as always—the English proletariat has always thought of itself as immensely superior to all other life-forms. I got a table for myself. As soon as I was reclined, I felt all the guilt and adrenaline shed. I bathed my face in a hot towel.

The format is that you are not allowed to use your hands for any operation. Instead, you are fed by a waitress who kneels beside you and feeds you with a pair of chopsticks. This neatly inverts the usual relationship between diner and server, because although the "service" is greatly increased, so too is the diner's helplessness. The Westerner, in particular, feels quite uncomfortable with this arrangement, because he is naturally inclined to think of service as subservience. Not so in Buddhist Asia. Here, service implies no ignominy at all. It is neutral, light. My server brought me *pla-duk*, catfish.

She cut it up for me and began parceling it out into my mouth as I lay there on one arm, trying to keep my head straight. The No-Hands experience was clearly surrounded by humor, little eruptions of embarrassment. When I tried to raise a napkin with my left hand, Lek cried, "Ah!" and stopped me. At that moment I thought back to McGinnis's complaints about Rome. Could one imagine a No-Hands Restaurant in Rome, what with spaghetti and pork crackling and so forth? Did they have No-Hands brothels here as well? They almost certainly did. I wondered if they had a No-Hands bank. That would be a better idea.

I began to enjoy it. It was the feeling of interconnectedness, and the first realization that loneliness was not the right word to describe the *farang*'s isolation in Bangkok. The *farang* is in reality not alone because Buddhists themselves seem not to believe in loneliness.

On the single TV screen, meanwhile, there appeared an image from a different universe: a mosque, in front of which a Thai Muslim stood being interviewed, a look of tense fury in his face. Then a road, a ruined house, burn marks along walls. A Thai army unit strolled through the main street of a village. A suddenly gathering unease in those images, with the sound turned off, the palms of the far south waving in a hurricane wind. Heads had been cut off in revenge attacks, as well as hands.

And there are times, too, when looking into the street you remember how recent all that commercial hedonism is. Bangkok made her fortune with the Vietnam War, for it was that war that made her into a pleasure capital. She was once surrounded by wars, dictatorships, Communist genocides, and she put herself forward as the slutty Cinderella of South

Asian cities, the only one where there was order, pleasure, no-hands restaurants, and a capable branch of the CIA. And now there was a new war, but this time it was internal and therefore something of a secret. The Muslims in the South were beginning to stir.

Lek lowered rolls of *guaytio* noodles toward my lips, and I noticed that each mouthful was carefully watched by the other *farang*s gathered there. The men in the Arsenal shirts watched this manuever closely, licking their lips. For them, it was a pornography of servitude. They had a whole lexicon for these girls. LBFM, for example. "Little brown fucking machines." It was sometimes difficult to be in the same room as these people, over whom, I thought, these aristocratic women lorded it with a natural, supple superiority. They must have thought of the men as "big white fucking machines," and only the mutual bawdy humor saved them both from a very severe critique. Lek then said something interestingly chauvinistic.

"You European, you always put down your glass like this."

And she slammed down the beer glass at my table.

•

The Buddhist idea of the self is dependent on the doctrine of *annata*, which means "the absence of self." Nothing in the universe has isolated selfhood because nothing is truly alone. A mind arises only because it is entangled with other beings, and Buddhists call this web of connectedness "dependent arising."

It's a startling idea, that there is no self lodged inside one's nervous system. That there is only a web of things which causes everything to arise. The individual's life is a dream dominated by unconscious chain reactions. A man and a dog are not so different, feeling their ways through sex and thirst, summers and winters, old age and death. They both know suffering, that all-important Buddhist idea known as *dukkha*. They both have little to hope for.

As the Buddha put it, with his supple and disarming realism: "Look to your own salvation, and with diligence." It is the same prophet who, when asked what he was, answered modestly, and without any reference to a divine lineage, "I am awake."

But there is one objection to Buddhism which we cannot get over. If I do not believe in reincarnation, why struggle to achieve something—freedom from desire and suffering—which will happen anyway when I die? Won't that happen soon enough, and won't the annihilation be total, everlasting, and completely satisfactory? It's strange that no religion can accept the finality of death and plan accordingly—except Taoism.

I went almost every night to the hotel bars, and especially when my check finally came. I particularly liked the Nai Lert Park and the Grand Hyatt on Ploenchit. The Nai Lert Park for its ancient gardens traversed by ponds and its grove of phallic lingams devoted to the earth goddess Tuptim, and the Grand Hyatt for its underground wine bar ensconsed inside a blown-up pastiche that looks from the outside like the British Museum coated with white chocolate. I suppose I am attracted to grandiosity, especially false grandiosity. In that respect I am quite Thai in my tastes.

At the Nai Lert I wandered around the gardens without spending a penny, sifting through the lagoons and islands in search of chance encounters or just a snatch of overheard conversation. The hotel was always full of glamorous people, but it also offered anonymity. There were frequent trade receptions, social dances. A hotel is like a train, a place where you can lie about yourself to your heart's content. You can tell a man sitting next to you that you are the Baron of Prinzapolka, and he might well believe you purely because you are both on a train. I noticed that these Bangkok functions were filled with frauds and pranksters, Westerners on the lam who were free to make up whatever they wanted about themselves. There were lords and princes and barons left, right, and center, and the Asians couldn't tell if they were real or not. A *farang* is a *farang*. Legion were the number of people here who had fled from home after staging fake deaths or other insurance scams. There was even a well-known American detective based in Thailand and in New York by the name of Byron Bales who specialized in tracking them down.

With time I perfected the art of extracting drinks from these characters, because their vanity is boundless and they need a listener at their side. They'll buy you a drink or four. You can find them at any hotel bar, dressed in kilts and windbreakers, tuxedos and corduroys, in ill-fitting shorts and Indian-made suits, their faces like smashed pumpkins, the right hand shaking, of course, their ties askew. They are like colonial officials in an awkward posting. Their thoughts are clear. Nice girls, treacherous natives, bloody awful weather. I was sure that I was beginning to look like them, because whenever I sat down at one of the bars in the Sheraton Grande, for example, or the Westin on the other side of Sukhumvit, or at the Black Horse at Asoke, they would lift their eyes for a moment and say, "Wotcha," as if I were a known factor. At the Nai Lert they were the grander imposters, and they would always try to sell you something, usually themselves. Tall, thin men in lovely suits would shake my hand and say "Lord Coggan," or "Viscount Bellamy," until my accent made them think I might be on to them and they slipped away with a little laugh. On occasion, I tried to pull off the same thing myself. It was surprisingly easy with Asians and Americans. It was as if the grandiosity of the hotel decors, all the chandeliers and the gold railings, the Intakul-designed flowers and the bowls of toasted nuts made this parade of deception easier.

There were those times when McGinnis put in his bou-

tonniere and took me as a guest to the British Club, to which
he had made his employer buy him a yearly membership.
Although its fees are modest and its facilities even humbler,
the British Club brought out all his arrogance, and on its
premises he went into a brief Flashman mode, yelling at people and doing jackknife dives into the pool. The club, however, did not possess the inflexible codes or the haughty
atmosphere which would have made such behavior funny. It
was delightfully matey and faintly seedy: perfectly British,
perhaps without knowing it. The squash courts and pool
area were like a Butlin's holiday camp in the Britain of the
early seventies. Massages were available from an old couple—"blind," as the members added. The clubhouse itself
was a trim white villa with dark-blue shutters. Inside, a
wainscoted lobby with oils of the queen and a slightly dusty
droplet chandelier made you feel deliciously oppressed at
once. Behind was a decrepit cricket ground bordered with
thickets of bamboo. On the ground floor of the clubhouse,
meanwhile, stood the Churchill Bar, with a frosted-glass
image of the old bastard and his cigar. Last orders at
10:00 p.m.—in Bangkok!—and rows of sports shields above
the bar itself. We would sometimes stand there dead drunk
and try to decipher them. The Hong Kong Football Club,
the University of Edinburgh, the Harlequin Football Club,
at whose shield McGinnis would often point with a terrible ginned-up finger and say, "Those boys have my motto
exactly. *Numquam dormio*!"

The drink to have here was of course the gin and tonic,
but gin and tonics made McGinnis impossible, as he sat by
the pool under the parasols and boasted of all the Bangkok
characters he knew and who knew him: "Shrimp" Chau-

vain, for example, the diminutive Englishman notorious for photographing hundreds of barely legal girls in the backstreets of the city and turning them into calendars. But I was pretty sure that he didn't know Chauvain, and that the tall stories of him and Shrimp on the rampage were versions of things he had heard in bars and remodeled to suit his own purposes. Shrimp's stories are local lore; McGinnis had latched on to them as he remade himself, cell by cell, as failures do when they have reached a certain age.

One day as we were sitting at the pool, pretending to be successes, a Thai attendant came up to us and said, *wai*'ing politely and bowing, that Mr. McGinnis's membership was no longer current, that it had been suspended for "nonpayment." He regretted that as of that time he would be unable to serve us any further drinks, or anything else for that matter, and that furthermore Mr. McGinnis and his guests would no longer be permitted to use the grounds of the British Club. He made some expressions of regret, of embarrassment, but none of them were capable of damping the rage that now burst out of McGinnis. A failure who has been slighted is far worse than a woman scorned, especially a British failure who is being asked to leave the British Club, which in terms of its facilities is one of the most cramped in Bangkok.

He drew himself up, as failed men do when they have been slighted in a mortal way. We were hardly alone at the pool. A dozen much more successful Britishers looked up coolly from their newspapers, because everything had been overheard. Their look was that measured sadism held back to the point of complete reticence that the British have perfected when witnessing the misfortunes of a man they have judged to be annoying. "You fucking limies," McGinnis began.

McGinnis's failure consisted of an inability to work with group dynamics. He wanted so badly to belong to this group, but as soon as they snubbed him his real hatred for them exploded. It was eloquent, as tirades against one's own people always are. Unlike hatred, self-hatred is perceptive. I later realized that McGinnis's membership had been suspended because he had been fired from Cyclex and was living on his savings. "Look at them all," he whispered to me on his way out. "None of them has had a hard-on in a decade. They're all drunks. Fat, badly dressed drunks. We're the ugliest men on planet Earth. Only our women are uglier. All right, I'm going. There's no cunt in here, anyway. None. I'm going back to Maida Vale."

"Goodbye, sir," a smiling manager said to us.

"I am joining the French Club today," McGinnis cried.

"There is no French Club, sir."

"Well, the Danish Club."

"I don't believe there's a Bangkok Danish Club, sir."

"All right, the Eden Club."

"I hope you have a wonderful time there, sir."

"They have what you don't have—namely, splendid cunt!"

I heard a shocked Thai waiter say to the receptionist, as if behind a hand, "Sounds anti-British to me, sir."

So it was farewell to our only bastion of home, a place so over-the-top in its Britishness that it threw the entire exercise of being an exile into vivid relief. Farewell to those lofty paintings upstairs of the *First Journey of the Victory*, to the illustrations of the Uniforms of the Scots Guards 1971, to

the Wordsworth Lounge and beef-and-barley soup. Farewell
to baked avocado prawn mornay in the Churchill Bar and
last orders at ten; farewell to the trophies of the Floodlight
Tournament and the Chairman Cup, the Rysecombe Cup
and the Davidson Cup, the *clock* of cricket balls under the
mango trees and the sight of the Jack flapping above the
whitewashed terrace.

But meanwhile I wondered why McGinnis always mentioned the Eden Club, as if the Eden was some sort of reference for him, and why he never hesitated to point out that
Shrimp Chauvain kept a John Wayne costume there. At this
point, however, I didn't ask him what he did at the Eden
Club. I wanted it to be a dark spot in the mind, a place I'd
get to eventually when I had degraded a bit.

•

I went to Lumpini Park as the mornings got hotter and the
rainy reason approached. It reminded me of the London
parks I grew up with, Lammas Park in Ealing, or Walpole
Park opposite it. The park is a Victorian idea, generous and
nostalgic, and new ones will be few and far between. It
expresses a view of human nature which has passed away.
Strolling, promenading, doing nothing but taking the air,
admiring bushes and flowers. But also simply breathing,
thinking, and occasionally committing suicide: the park is a
place where one does all aimless things that one should be
doing anyway. Or it was. Now hordes of joggers tear around
the paths, assemblies of the elderly do their Tai Chi on the
lawns, and schoolkids pass out on *yaa baa* under the trees.
The noble park has rapidly become squalid.

I came in the morning to read the papers, and then again

at night. At that time the park, named after Buddha's birth-
place in Nepal, was filled with karaoke machines. I couldn't
have imagined a park filled with karaoke machines, or seen
the point, but there they were. Lumpini resounded to the din
of karaoke machines. I walked around the two slime-green
lakes, the Chinese Style Clock Tower, and the Outdoor Gym.
There were men sitting by the paths having their hair cut,
fingering mahjong boards, sleeping on mats. There were
long lines of people doing group aerobics, hundreds of them
all synchronized together, and there was a moment in the
day that I relished above all others, the moment when the
National Anthem was played at 6:00 p.m. The National
Anthem was composed by the king and sounds like a Maoist
marching hymn of the forties. When it is played every day at
six, everyone has to freeze, stop in their tracks, and observe
a respectful minute of immobility. In the Outdoor Gym, men
stopped with their weights in midair, their faces contorted;
the aerobics groups and the Tai Chi practitioners similarly
went into suspended animation. It was like a spell. And one
could keep walking all the same, the only moving person
in the whole park, the only animate man among the spell-
bound.

After the National Anthem, I walked down to the Suan
Lum Night Market, entertained by the hookers of both sexes
who patrol the park's perimeter fence, women to the east,
men to the west. The metallic, inelegant towers of Rama IV
Road faded into the soft hour of menace that brings in tropical nights, and a surcharge of electric light burst out of the
air. The human face turns colorless in this light, the eyes
look rapid and overexcited. I passed through the Night Market with light fingers and indifferent appetite. I was rarely

tempted by the Thai rock bands in the beer garden and the tourist pavilions of "Ayutthaya antiques," though I must admit I was drawn for some reason to the tawdry reproduction of an ancient Khmer library made of fiberglass which served as the HQ of the market's Tourist Police. I passed through this gatelike structure, through its gold spotlights, and remembered that Suan Lum would soon be razed to the ground to be replaced by a hotel, a mall, and an exhibition center. It was a thought worth holding for a moment: this fake reproduction of the past would soon be consigned to the actual past.

I sometimes went to Safari Steak opposite the Joe Louis Puppet Theater or the Seafood Plaza at the market's northern edge near the Lumpini boxing stadium, after which I could wander through the Plant Nursery and then go to watch the early bouts of *muay thai* at the stadium. I loved the Lumpini stadium not for the boxing itself but for the mulberry trees of great age looming over the outdoor cafés around it. They cast shadows which reminded me of summer days, and one could sit under them for hours without remembering for a moment that it was night.

On the first day of Songkran, Farlo took me to Silom. We sat in Barbican, in Patpong, one of my favorite bars in Bangkok, while water bombs and wet flour filled the air, and he told me about his marriage and his financial affairs, which were more complicated than could be imagined. With a forgiving sadness I tried to imagine where I would be in my late fifties: here, in Asia, married to a peasant girl in Cambodia, doing what Farlo did? We sat next to an Australian couple, and from time to time he leaned over and said, "May I ask if you've considered a peaceful break in the Cardamom Mountains in Cambodia? None of this, like." He motioned to the street above. "Just tigers and a few land mines. There's nae golf but I can take ye shooting deer with automatic weapons. The name's Mickey. I have my own place in the foothills. Clean water. English spoken. Four separate bird-watching accommodation towers. I'll do ye a rate." And he passed them his card, which read *Cardamom Adventures*. "The wife's local. She cooks a mean *lok-lok*."

From the basement windows, the largely Japanese street was revealed at knee level—the black façade of the Aoyama Club, the Alpha Member Club with girls in ball gowns, Milano and the Enjoy Club, and Marmelade. Outside Pandora the girls held out menus of services to men stepping out of wet limos. Farlo looked around at the bottles of wine in casements along the walls and the small film noir paintings with wide-open and slightly disbelieving eyes. He never seemed quite at home in Bangkok. His hands, crossed over each other on the black tabletop, looked completely Khmer, like those of a farmer in the region where he lived. His thumb itched. He said "Ay" a lot, shaking his head instead of nodding it. "Ay, another day of love. That's what my old lady says every morning. She says it in Khmer and it sounds good."

The Songkran crowds swelled. Mama-sans stood by the doors with nightmare faces, under notices in *kanji* which neither Thai nor *farang* would understand. The subtle segregation of races, of languages, as if each has their erotic proclivities which cannot mix. "You can't be sad here," I thought aloud. "Infuriated, but not sad." It was a geisha district bathed in the color red, and that fleshy color settled inside the mind like a soothing reminder of the body's placidity.

That night, McGinnis was taking us to a party. We were going to meet him on Suriwong. We walked for a mile. Under shady trees like those of a European boulevard, down crooked Soi Tarntawan, where the smoke of roasting corn filled the air, past the Solid Club and doorways of half-sleeping girls, until we came to the streets of gay clubs with their predictable names: Fresh Boy and Balls, Hair Gay and Love Me Tender. We went into Boys Town for a while and watched lads in white underwear dancing on a small stage. I noticed the sign for Balls, which I had seen from a taxi a few weeks before. It turned out to be a comfortable sports bar with a lovely shrine next to it. It had an outdoor terrace at which sportily dressed middle-aged *farang* men sat calmly with their boys.

As we sat at Balls, McGinnis appeared through the density of the crowd, drenched with wet flour and holding a wet cigarette that was still lit in one hand. He was dressed in a linen outfit that now clung to his body like cellophane, and the hairs of his chest showed through a soaked blue shirt.

"Did you know," I said to Farlo quickly, "that he got fired?"

"I didn't know he was employed."

"Cyclex Refrigeration Systems?"

"I looked them up, lad. They don't exist. He has a small stipend from his family, I think. He also sells birds."

"Sells birds?"

"Ay. Import-export to China."

"There can't be any money in selling birds."

"Why don't you ask him?"

McGinnis came up puffing, his hair dripping with flour. Along Suriwong large *farang*s, probably British or Dutch, swaggered with plastic water cannons. They could shoot pedestrians on the far side of the boulevard with ease, and they had got McGinnis with ease.

"There must be a case," he drawled, "for the withdrawal of passports."

The cigarette glowed in his drenched hand.

"Hello, boys," he said loudly, casting an eye at the sign. "So it's cocktails at Balls, eh?"

"We thought it looked a nice place," Farlo said.

"Look at my wet suit. I got this made for me at an Indian tailor called Beethoven. So it's a Beethoven suit. I am at Balls in a Beethoven suit."

In the taxi, he sat between us and said to the driver, "*Roong muu, Klong Tuey,*" an address we had never heard

of. Klong Tuey is the city's port, behind which lies a massive
ghetto. We passed through the gray streets near Chong
Nonsi, heading for Rama IV, and I was now getting used to
the ragged avenues with their metal shutters, their hungry-
looking mango trees, and their glints of fire. They made me
think of New York fifteen years ago, twenty years ago, the
Bowery in 1983, when I first walked down it high on psilo-
cybin. McGinnis took out a flask from an inner pocket and
uncorked it. I took a quick swig: it tasted like a medicinal
syrup. We passed along the brightest part of Sukhumvit, and
there are times when you remember that it's the longest
street in the world, that it reaches all the way from downtown Bangkok to the Cambodian border.

There were new gyms there that were just opening, L.A.-
style fitness palaces with techno music projected onto the
street. Through high windows, the joggers, the ponytails
bobbing on treadmills. The statues of gods and goddesses
stood lit up with a creamy kitchiness, piled high with
marigolds, while cranes and scaffolding soared up on either
side. A long street bordered by a canal led down to Rama IV
and into the area around Bangkok University.

•

Along one side of the Bangkok University campus lies a
waterway known locally as *Guai nam thai*, after the Thai
word for banana, *guai*. No one seems sure of the exact
translation. "Banana forest"? Perhaps once upon a time
banana boats unloaded their cargo there; or else it had once
been a banana grove. On the other side there is a bridge not
far from the campus gates, and beyond it lies the port and
the walled slums. The railway for the container port runs
along its perimeter wall, and the tracks themselves have with

time turned into a ghetto, with shacks nailed together on either side.

For months I had been only dimly aware of this sprawling zone, noting its presence in passing when I skimmed through crime stories in the *Bangkok Post*. There was nothing in it to see, no restaurants to slum in, no bars, no oddities to linger over. Late at night, I sometimes glimpsed it from a taxi as I shot along the expressway, and suddenly there was a twinkling of open fires down there, signs of life coming from a different city which was now half submerged by progress. Streets, markets, kitchens, none possessing a name I knew. So it appeared like a black hole, but in reality it was just the far side of the class divide. By the port, where the slums were separated from the city by a real wall, you could see that much of it was more or less jungle, with people living in shacks and tree houses, or sleeping in trees. It had been there for decades, neglected and feared, but over the shabby gates to this underworld there were sometimes signs in English which read "Welcome!" as if people here, too, had their internationalist pride to consider.

These walled-off neighborhoods surrounded the container port which employed their inhabitants as day laborers. Some were warrens of streets with self-built houses, squatter camps where the slaughterhouse workers lived, or crazy piles made of random materials where dozens of families endured—the men living off homemade *yaa baa*, which they sold in the city.

•

Roong muu is the city slaughterhouse, buried inside a mixed Thai-Viet slum: only these impoverished Catholics could kill animals, an act forbidden to the Buddhists who happily ate their flesh. It lay next to the *roong gung*, the place where they slaughter millions of shrimp all night long.

The killing of animals is secretive in Bangkok, and I wondered how McGinnis had found this place, which most Bangkokians had never visited. I noticed now the slaughterhouse workers idled around the low, metal-roofed buildings with the look of men who are stoned and who will be killing pigs with hammers all night long. To get them through it they are said to take drugs which are made inside the slum itself. Mostly, you will hear, it is *yaa baa*, a methamphetamine mixed with caffeine, but sometimes also the underground drug 505. The most terrifying of these is a substance called *sii qun roi*, which in Thai means "four by one hundred."

Pig blood running through the gutters appears a dark blue, like the tattoos that cover the skins of the killers themselves: Five Buddhas, spirit tigers, and blue *yantas*. Such tattoos are called *roi sak*, and protect the wearers. Sometimes they form the letters of vedic spells written in the ancient Khmer script called *khom*, using an ink made from lampblack and Indian sepia mixed with sap and lizard skin. Some tattooists even add the chin fat of human corpses, of people who have died violent deaths.

Pigs are highly intelligent, and they know what's in store for them, but nevertheless they are fatalistic. What good would a breakout do? And then Farlo got up and started dancing, turning slowly on his heels, his arms akimbo. The killers found it hilarious. But what was going on inside that haunted head? Like me, had he started to remember the killing in other places, other times, the pleasure of it so deftly hidden afterward by excuses? What about the spirit of the gecko?

Afterward, we went for a walk around the giant shrimp

warehouses, where McGinnis put a hand to his ear and said, "Can you hear them? The shrimp are screaming. Boiled alive, and no one cares. So much for Buddhism!"

•

Sii qun roi is made from the active ingredient in mosquito coils, an insecticide called parathin which is manufactured by the Heibei Long Age Pesticide Company in Hengshui City, China. According to the company, parathin efficiently kills all kinds of plant parasites on rice, cotton, and corn, including cotton aphids, fruit moths, and mites. It is phytotoxic on melons, however, and is forbidden for use on tea trees.

Parathin is mixed with a marijuana-like smokeable leaf indigenous to Thailand called *bai krathom*, which is then added to soda, the muscle relaxant alprazolam (Xanax), and cough syrup. The result is a drug which is now classified by the Thai military as a "mind control substance." It is used by Muslim guerrillas in the south to brainwash potential suicide bombers.

I later found out that McGinnis got his *yaa baa* from Klong Tuey as well. He would serve them up at teatime, reddish-orange, green, or purple tablets flavored with grape, orange, and vanilla, like children's sweets and marked with either the letters R or WY. He would say, "I call it my *Fliegeschokolade*." "Flying chocolate" was the term Luftwaffe pilots gave to the methamphetamine-spiked chocolate they sucked down during long bombing missions.

•

There are color-coded maps created by the UN that show which drugs are most popular in the world's nations. In Asia, cannabis dominates both Australia and Indonesia. Heroin is the drug of choice in China and Vietnam, while ATs (amphetamines) prevail in Thailand, Cambodia, Laos, and Japan. In Thailand, ATs are the drug of the young, marketed as candy-like tablets, but also smoked by heating the tablet on a square of foil in a rite known as "chasing the dragon."

The whole country is awash with it. People eat it in the clubs, in the massage parlors, on the street, in university libraries, in exam halls. It was banned in Thailand in 1970, but there is a curious story behind its name. It used to be called *yaa maa*, or "horse medicine," because that was the name of the company which manufactured it. In 1996, the then–minister of health, Sanoh Thienthong, renamed it *yaa baa*, or "madness drug," to scare off young users. He couldn't have made a more naïve blunder. As soon as it was dubbed "madness drug," demand exploded. In deference to its distant origin, it was also called "Nazi speed."

I stopped sleeping when taking *yaa baa*, and went down to the pier, unable to close my eyes. In the rainy season it is often ninety at midnight, but the rain is soothing. Through the windows of the Spaniard's ground-floor apartment, meanwhile, I noticed large canvases propped against a wall, a few candles burning with a bohemian aspiration, and from time to time a naked form pacing back and forth holding a book, reading upright and rocking himself like a Torah scholar. He seemed as jittery as I did, another European naked in the heat. But the privacy of strangers was the premise of being *farang* in Bangkok, the guarantee of being left alone.

•

There was something fantastical in the Slaughterhouse neighborhood: people sleeping like lemurs in trees, paths cutting through a forest made of compacted trash. McGinnis knew them all. He took me down some that passed through deeper jungle, with spirit houses built by the addicts in honor of their own demons. Some of these shrines had plastic dolls inside them, toy cars, syringes, or photographs from magazines. We passed shacks where old couples lay together smoking, their hands raised in greeting. And it began to dawn on me that I could possibly live here at some point in the future, because I could always live in any city that has a neighborhood like the Slaughterhouse.

On my last night, however, I went with McGinnis to somewhere very different—the Trimurthi shrine near Central World Plaza, to see the crowds looking for luck in love. The shrine is devoted to the color red, as if red were the color of love, and its godhead is the Hindu *trimurthi* triad of Vishnu-Brahma-Shiva. With its lush red decorations, the shrine itself has a Valentine's aura, and the crowd bristling with red roses seems to believe in the karma of love with an intensity and naïveté which can take you by surprise in a city which is so casual about the body. Women plead to the trinity to increase their libido and fertility; couples wanting babies gather round to make their votive offerings.

I was struck by the face of Brahma, because it's a face you rarely see. In India there are only three temples to Brahma, and he is the least visibly worshiped of all Hindu gods. Bangkok, however, seems to receive him and relish him. We walked down to the more famous Erawan shrine, and there it is Brahma alone who commands the neighborhood. With his four faces, he gazes out at the new century embodied in shopping malls with an elegant indifference. None of Brahma's four arms ever carries a weapon, an unusual thing for an Indian god. Instead, he carries scepters and spoons brimming with holy ghee and coconuts filled with holy water. But Brahma is a god cursed by love—it was desire, the pursuit of a woman, that undid him and which explains why he is so unpopular in India. At least I heard this from McGinnis, who added: "It's the same reason he is so popular with Thais."

Brahma is the creator of the universe. While engaged in this monumental task, he also created a female god called Shatarupa, "one with a hundred beautiful forms." He immediately became infatuated with her, and, alarmed by his attentions, she moved about restlessly, to avoid his gaze. To keep this alluring goddess within his sight, however, Brahma developed five heads, four on the sides and one on top, so that he became a divine periscope of lust, an all-seeing cosmic voyeur.

Shiva cut off Brahma's top head to control him. He felt that Brahma's infatuation was distinctly incestuous, that Shatarupa was, in a manner of speaking, Brahma's daughter. Shiva restricted the worship of Brahma as a sign of his disgrace, and ever since, the repentant god has been reciting the four Vedas.

Brahma's own life cycle defines the life and death of whole universes. A single day or night of Brahma's life lasts 4,320,000,000 years, and a whole twenty-four hours for this amazing, baffling god is the same as 8,640,000,000 years for us, which begs the question: How many days, how many billions of years, did his love for Shatarupa last? Could one more day of love be equivalent to so many countless centuries?

I traveled to Asia for work, covering psychiatry and science for American magazines, and I passed through Bangkok sporadically, in pursuit of research for medical articles which I could write in hotel rooms. Each time I went, the city had changed. I took in the opening of the Skytrain or the rising height of the billboards upon which iPods and sneaker brands and Italian swimwear appeared like fresh fruit, proving the city's desperate desire to be more contemporary than anywhere.

Here capitalism had been imposed upon new ground and was itself novel. A capitalism that was not merely "Asian" but Indochinese, Hindu-Buddhist, Sino-Malay. All along Sukhumvit Road the Skytrain stations had appeared, lifted above the street on cement columns, their arcades bright with organic fruit juice vendors, opticians, and travel agents. They were new urban spaces, cleaner and wider than those of the city below them. It was as if after centuries of chaos the city was yearning for geometry and order, and she was getting her wish.

There were times when I took a room for a week at one of the cheaper places on Soi 4 and tried to trace the men who had all left the Primrose and settled elsewhere. I rarely found them. I went to the dental clinic on Soi 49, had my crowns and fillings done, and then spent evenings alone playing pool with Arab punters at the Grace Hotel, a place that satisfies their every need.

I spent many nights wandering around Little Arabia on Soi 3/1, going to Al Ferdoss in the Schiller Inn to smoke a water pipe and watch the men in lamb's wool hats and djellabas filing with tarts through the lobby next to the dining room. Eating a fatoosh salad with an orange shish and watching such maneuvers, or simply taking in the restaurants with displays of plastic veal chops where men in tattersail jackets cry "Lam', Lam' " all night long.

The small elephants of Southeast Asia plod by with boys seated on their heads, ice picks dug into the animals' ears, because it is the elephants who do the begging and charming here. And I daresay one can be happy watching a Russian pilot stuffing his face with slices of watermelon, or scanning the crinkled posters of Crusader castles in Lebanon or the Thai ketchup bottles and plastic orchids that rise from the tables.

At four in the morning in the midst of Little Arabia, in all its steam and filth, the face of a painted *kathoey*, a transgender boy-girl thick with rosebud paint, appears through the neons with a scornful little smile. It is the Thai cult of beauty, mannered, like the art of puppetry.

A photographer based in Bangkok once said to me, "It is difficult here because of their obsession with beauty. They are the most beauty-obsessed people on earth. But it can't be photographed."

I began to change rooms from night to night, just to spread myself as widely as possible over the city. I remember rooms on Petchaburi Road, in hotels like the Livingstone and the Amari Watergate; hovels near Silom sprayed every night with insecticide. For a while I favored the Livingstone, on a small street off Sukhumvit 33. Its entrance was flanked by two enormous elephant tusks, and inside the decor was African Thatch. There was a sinister pool and a bar staffed with nymphs.

•

There were times, too, when my medical trips to and from Bangkok threw that city into a strange relief. One of these was an expedition to Borneo to investigate an obscure mental illness known in Malay as *latah*. *Latah* is a "culture-bound syndrome," a mental illness which is specific to a single culture. In the *American Diagnostic Manual* it is listed as a "hyper-startle syndrome": when a human being is surprised by a loud noise, he or she will go into a momentary trance. Typically they will flap their arms in a characteristic way, noticeable only in a slow-motion film, and utter a sexual obscenity of some kind. Technically, they go into a split-second state of hypnosis.

In Malaysia this momentary trance is experienced differently by old women, and by old women alone. For them the experience extends to half an hour, an hour, and sometimes even longer. No one knows why.

Kuching, in Sarawak, is even hotter than Bangkok— a sluggish town built around a dark green river. There's a strong Chinese presence in coastal Sarawak, but the Dayak presence is equally evident. The British were here, as evidenced by their squat cream arcades, but they didn't have the energy to build seriously. From there I drove to Lundu, on the border of Indonesia. It's even hotter than Kuching, a place of torpor and bewilderment dominated by Chinese merchants. I had spent some wonderful afternoons in Kuching with the anthropologist Peter Kedik as we met women in the suburbs who claimed they had been made *latah* by being *poked too much*. "Repressed sex," Kedik would say as we drank hot chocolate with them in their sitting rooms. We watched them jump up and down on one leg like pogo sticks, shocked into a *latah* fit by a simple clap of hands. I think both of us felt a surprising calm before this scene, but Kedik had studied it many times. "The old men, you see, have an outlet for their sexual drives. They can always go to some discreet brothel somewhere. But the women, after a certain age—"

Outside Lundu, my Iban driver found us a place called Kampung Seberang, a small village straddling the road. He knew of a family named Suut whose grandmother was *latah*. When the woman's son brought in a black cat and slipped it behind her, she went into a seizure. Imitating the sumo on the screen, she put her own foot into a wrestling lock and rolled on the floor in a ball. I asked the driver what she was shouting and, mortified, he leaned down to my ear. "She is saying 'cock,' sir. 'Cock.' It is what she is saying. 'You fuck me big fat cock,' sir. I am sorry to say."

It is what *latah* ladies always say. The trance opens a sexual door through which all the mind's debris flows, and the mind of a Dayak grandmother and a white sex tourist in Bangkok are essentially the same.

•

I traveled around Malaysia, to Penang and Kuala Lumpur, always looking for doctors who would talk to me about *latah*.

One night the doctor I was interviewing took me with his wife to the village of Kampung Kuantan, just outside Kuala Selangor, on the Selangor River. The couple were youngish ethnic Malays, conscientious Muslims, with an oddball, sultry charm heightened by their buttoned-down fashion sense; he had interned at Addenbrooks Hospital in Cambridge and spoke an English that was far too perfect by half. The river is narrow, running between jungles, and Malaysians came there to watch the famous synchronized fireflies, which they call *kelip kelip*. Indians punt you down the river on long boats, wielding their poles with suave expertise, and saying, "Look, fireflies," every time a firefly appears, which is every five seconds. The doctor and his wife lounged in our boat like figures from Renoir, except that there was no sun. I told them about *latah* in Sarawak, and they looked at each other in amusement.

"You don't understand much about Asia," the doctor said. "You may have thought you saw something called *latah*, but you didn't."

"You mean it was a show?"

"Not necessarily. But that doesn't mean that Western medicine has identified it correctly. You have been reading Ronald Simons of the University of Wisconsin, have you not?"

I stammered, "But he is the authority."

"Not here he isn't. Here in Malaysia we do not all read Ronald Simons. Not at all. We do not necessarily think that *latah* even exists. We think that madness exists, though."

"But those old ladies? You mean they are just mad."

"Dayaks, my friends. It's another world."

"Is it really another world?"

But they were adamant. "We Malays," the wife said gravely, "would never behave like that." She lowered her voice. "Cock?"

"Oh, Miriam, really."

But what about *koro*? *Koro* is the delusion that your penis is being made to retract inside your body until it has disappeared altogether. It is disappearing-penis syndrome, and is related to "penis-theft syndrome" in some parts of Africa, in which men believe that their penis has been stolen through witchcraft. People were jailed for penis theft in Nigeria. A prison had even been stormed by penis-theft victims when one of the so-called witches had been held there. But everyone concerned still had his penis, of course.

Koro existed all over Southeast Asia but was most famous in Malaysia. Singapore's infamous race riots in 1969 were reputed to have erupted when Malay men suspected Chinese influence in their disappearing penises.

The doctor coughed politely.

"That is all past and done with. There is absolutely no more *koro* in Malaysia, I can assure you. If there was I would have heard of it."

"Isn't it illegal?" the wife asked.

"It is," he said uncertainly.

So, I thought, our cocks are safe from the Chinese. We punted on silently, the *kelip kelip* flickering on and off in synchronicity, and the subject of stolen and disappearing penises was quietly dropped.

"Sir," the punter cried, "fireflies!"

Through a Bangkok monsoon I tracked down Dennis to a condo tower on Sukhumvit Soi 24, a street so long that you cannot walk the length of it and back in a single evening. He lived far down it, close to Seafood Town, where he liked to eat every evening, with his cane, his shades, and a high-culture paperback, immersed in an Asian crowd and surrounded by bubbling fish tanks, determinedly lost to the outside world.

There was something of an Old Testament figure about him, even though he was always clean-shaven—or shaven, anyway. This establishment has a great sign slung across the street, so that you feel as if the street belongs to the restaurant and not the other way around. At night, the red letters *Seafood* burn across it, and I wondered what had drawn the dry Australian to such a touristy street. His building was studded with fairy lights and shone like a shabby Christmas tree. It was inhabited mostly by single men, alone with their fridges of Johnnie Walker and their Carrefour shopping bags, and through its papery walls you could hear the dismal sound of heavy metal.

Dennis, too, was alone, in a three-room unit with almost no furniture, the kitchen filled with bottles and the front room converted into a watercolor studio. He seemed to prefer a shambolic setup, inside which he could sew together his paintings and his long reading sessions. A sober study in the

Life Alone. His marriage seemed to have slipped away from him altogether, like a memory that cannot be reassembled after an irrevocable break with the past. He looked a little frailer, however. As we sat there, smoking and peering through a small window into the vegetation of the condo garden, I had the feeling that a switch had been thrown inside him, and that he had decided to make these rooms his final resting place.

He took me down in the elevator, his cane tapping the floor like the feeler of a large beetle (an effect augmented by his supersized aviators), and I told him about the trip to Lundu, the *latah*s of the forest, and in an incident where Mrs. Suut jumped up and down on one leg and invoked the male anatomy. "Christ," he said, shaking his head. "Freud was right, wasn't he, mate?" I said I wouldn't go that far.

"And look at you," he went on. "You're looking a bit seedy, Miss Lalant. What happened to your hair? Long, mate? You look like the Lord. You look like a seedy girl."

Your appearance decays and you don't notice anything, and as it decays your effect on others changes. We went through the glass doors of the lobby and I saw my wild, matted hair in a reflection and I felt its weight touching the bottom of my neck. Curious. Why had I not cut it as I usually do?

"The police will nick you," he said. "The Thai police hate hippies. They use cattle prods on them."

"It's an urban myth, Dennis. No one's going to use a cattle prod on me because of my hair."

"We'll see, mate."

"How's Porntit?"

"Ah, there's a story. And it's Porn*tip*, not *tit*."

"I never said it was *tit*."

"You went along with it, mate."

"I never called her Porntit. You did."

"Not me. You all called her Porntit, not me. You were hearing what you wanted to hear."

On the street the pedestrians walked in two orderly columns on either side. They were cowed by the heat, their faces custard-colored under the bombardment of neons. On the one hand, the massage parlors with their rows of shoes outside and their good-luck cats recall domesticity—and on the other, the fluorescent tubing forming a new kind of international English jolts the night walker's nervous system into a quiet anxiety. "Where am I?" he thinks. "And what kind of place is this? Is it mine or theirs?" With detachment, I watched Dennis tap his way down Soi 24 like Blind Pew in *Treasure Island*. He was off on an adventure, his nightly adventure one might say, and there was that vibrancy that is so touching in the nearly old when you see that the light in them has not yet died out and that they are *willing to go on*. We ate a lobster at Seafood Town, blinking in the brightness of its aerodrome dining hall, scorched by saucers of *naam phrik plaa*. His hand laid on the paper tablecloth twitching like a slug, the nails beveled by a salon girl. The skin of the old looks fragile and waxlike in a neon glare, as if suited only to the gentle forgiveness of daylight. Dennis looked around as he ate, and he told me that McGinnis had gone into the pineapple and mango juice export business, selling mostly to Russia and China.

"He's still after the boys, though."

"The boys?"

"Oh, he's notorious. Didn't you know?"

I asked where McGinnis was living, what his numbers were. One always wants to catch up with people.

"No idea. Everyone's a nomad here."

"And Farlo?"

"I had Christmas with him. He's catering to one tourist a year. It seems to keep him fully occupied. The missus in England is suing him."

"So life goes on."

"That's the best thing about it."

Then he added, "We're not like you. We're lifers."

It was the way they thought of themselves, in a tone of superiority and doom. "It's urban Tahiti," I thought. "And these are the seedy English sailors who have washed up on her shores."

They wanted to eat lotus, but when they finally tasted it, it made them uneasy. We walked along Soi 24. Past a Vishnu shrine with ceramic dancers inside it, their legs raised like Hindu can-can girls. They danced among elephants, horses, and gods. Rain flattened the street's dust and we sailed past the Impala Hotel, a spa called the Asia Herb Association, and the green neon of the Ariston Hotel, where Dennis liked to retreat for his after-dinner Sierra Tequila.

Having climbed its steep steps, we came into the Big Ben bar, with a line of cherry leather seats and a strawberry telephone. The lobby was empty but for a lone Japanese man asleep in one of the armchairs, forming a landscape of complete male solitude uninterrupted by any female laughter. So this was how lifers liked to spend their evenings, inconsolable at a bar with only the sound of rain in the background, with Cinzano ashtrays at their fingertips. Dennis looked like a fixed horse on a carousel, shiny and pink, as if he should be moving to mechanized gypsy music.

"It's a bloody awful place, isn't it?" he said, gesturing back toward the street, along which the usual soccer hooligans were winging their way with LBFMs on their arms. "But then again, it's better than any other place."

"Better than Queensland in winter? Better than Paris?"

"I can't talk about Paris, never been there. But better than Queensland, for Christ's sake."

"So it's not so awful, Dennis."

"Bloody hot, though."

"You could give up the nightlife and settle down."

"I can't give up the nightlife, mate. I can't give up the girls. If you give up the girls you're a dead man, aren't you?"

"You could find a girl in Perth."

"You're joking. A girl? No, a pensioner like me isn't finding anyone. Who would have me? That's the sad part. It's not very dignified, I know. I'm embarrassed. It's humiliating for a man my age—but it's better than being dead."

He began to describe his days and nights. They were a relentless quest for intimacy in which intimacy played almost no part. And quest was the right word. He got up, he said, at midday and painted in his apartment, listening to classical music. Then he went down to the cyber café on Soi 4 to check his stocks and view the CNN website. In Bangkok it was imperative to have habits or you quickly went crazy. You were alone in the heat, in the Buddhist whirl, and you had no bearings to keep you straight. You were a sinking ship and you had to keep bailing yourself out. And, he admitted, you kept sinking anyway.

He slept badly, he said. The AC kept him awake, and the air was suffocating at this time of year. What if he had a heart attack all alone in his little condo? He had nightmares about his wife. He passed his afternoons at the Marriott health club—a marvelous place, if I didn't know it. Best sauna in the city. It was popular with French perverts, whom he met convivially in the hot pool. He watched TV there for a while, then went down to the enormous Marriott bar for a Singapore Sling. It was retirement, you see, and there was nothing to do every day except *inform oneself* and pleasure oneself. Every day was the same. As dusk fell through the cathedral windows of the Marriott, he felt a rising gaiety, a mad exhilaration like the high of laughing gas.

"Pathetic" might be an angry word to describe his nightly wandering down Sukhumvit Road, and he might say "pitiful" instead, but either way he was now one of those *dirty old men*. But then, the old had a choice that couldn't be avoided. They could choose dignity, neutrality, and asexuality, of course, but mostly that dignity was chosen for them. They didn't go for it of their own accord, because no one in their right mind would: you can't let go of life just like that. However decrepit, the living are never asexual, and I thought back to Mrs. Suut in the jungles of Borneo. What I saw in her was the suffering that sex imposes on the old, the ugly. *Dukkha*. That, Dennis said, was what Buddhist hookers understood even better than himself: suffering. They sensed that it came directly from pleasure.

"I go to the corner of Sukhumvit," he said, "and stare at all the rich women buying silk handbags and ball gowns in Na Ra Ya, the chic store on that corner opposite the Botox clinic. They go from Skin Rejuvenation straight over to the Na Ra Ya to buy handbags. To each his vice, eh?"

He never went to the massage parlors clustered around the end of Soi 24, with names like Bee, Happiness, and Body Treat. What he liked was to walk up and down this section of Sukhumvit as far as the junction with Asoke, where the Westin Hotel stands, off the beaten path, along stretches of sidewalk which are much less well lit than the nightlife areas farther south. It was a mysteriously enjoyable area for him, full of *tight corners* which he did not know how to navigate. It was made up of crannies where the flow of the city came to a standstill but in which there were women who seemed to move in a dimension all their own. By the Westin, he said, there was a curious line of fir trees next to the pedestrian walkover, and before them a line of stores where peddlers and street sellers had their blankets, and where people played chess and checkers late at night. The girls here were not the most beautiful, admittedly, they were the ones you walked by almost without noticing, who rarely made a gesture at you.

It had taken him a while before he summoned up the courage to catch one of their eyes and linger behind the fir trees. He had his Thai phrases prepared. *Gii baht short time?* And here by the trees the rate was reasonable, and the answer would be *Nung paan*, one thousand. It was well known the old men were popular with the girls because they gave out quickly and were no trouble. He liked slipping his shaky hand into theirs, with a soft sweat exchanged, and winging off to the little by-the-hour hotel near Soi Cowboy. He enjoyed the sordidness of that place, the money, the formality, the way it was the same every time. He liked the way it was bare and simple, like a dance where you've memorized all the moves.

He had a dry humor about it, since he had no illusions about himself, and I heard in his tone all the qualities of the aging john that few will sympathize with, but which I must sympathize with. You either think life is jolly, positive, and under control, or you don't. "I could never understand the attraction of having a prostitute," Michael Myers is supposed to have said to his friend Graham Greene, who was a well-known fan of them. "It's like paying someone to beat you at tennis." But sometimes one wants to be beaten at silly games, one wants to know the sweetness of loss.

One night, soon after we had reestablished contact, McGinnis took me to a place on Ratchadaprisek Road called the White House, an entertainment complex whose main body is shaped like an Italian church. Spotted with sweat, dark patches on his shirt, his Loakes forsaken for open-toe sandals, McGinnis was nevertheless still quite well kempt for his age. On one of his breast pockets was a logo consisting of a garland of fruit and the circular legend *Sino-Thai Fruit Ideas*. He was clearly embarrassed by it, and explained it away at once. The company wasn't exactly his; it belonged to a Chinese friend who liked everyone to embody the team spirit. At least it didn't say "Everyone's a Leader" or "Together We Overcome." They paid his health insurance and he had a fair amount of time off to explore the parts of the pleasure industries so far untouched by his tireless odysseys. But I, for one, thought he looked changed, a little more drawn and hollowed-out, his eyes paler and more liquid, as if preparing to turn into oysters. To which he responded by saying, "You look the same, you little bitch! Younger, if anything. What are you on?"

For miles, Ratchada is lined by multistorey massage parlors: Caesar's next to the Swissotel, or else the Emerald or the Nataree, places with imposing entrances alive with droplet chandeliers. Machines of pleasure, large and humming and comfortable. Here your pleasure is measured, processed, extinguished with clockwork efficiency and a dash of hospitality. Libido is simply visible. There is something utopian about it, like something dreamed up by Charles Fourier in his ideal cities known as Phalansteries. All human needs catered for. "Is it possible," Cyril Connolly observed, "to love any human being without being torn limb from limb?" Yet sex, according to that unhappy Irish writer, was harmless. "No one was ever made wretched in a brothel. There need be nothing angst-forming about the sexual act. Yet a face seen in the tube can destroy our peace for the rest of the day—" Elsewhere, however, he expresses a more Christian mood: "As bees their sting, so the promiscuous leave behind them in each encounter something of themselves by which they are made to suffer."

One doesn't see such devastated faces here, in the clubs, the vast discos, the culs-de-sac of venues where the hipsters go. Ratchada is lit up like a city under aerial bombardment, because contemporary entertainment has something warlike about it, something of the frenzy of battle.

Nightfall. The arc lamps of the construction sites flicker on. The waste lots are busy with soccer games and at the corners of the *soi*, beanpole girls in nightclub dresses wait for their boyfriends. Before going into the White House we sat for a while inside the bright neon box of Somboon Seafood, drinking Chinese tea and looking down from the second-floor windows. I liked the hesitant motions of lonely men walking through their own vacuums to get to a massage parlor, the way the green neons of the massage parlors themselves suddenly came on, as if remembering something. I admired this impersonality, because it was my sort of impersonality, and I was tired of churches in Europe, and brownstones and parks and stone beauty in general.

The "church" was actually a seafood market whose entrance was lit up by a twenty-foot model of a crayfish. Inside lay a dining room with a hundred tables. The dome itself was decorated with pink neon piping, like an inverted cake, and painted with a fishbowl scene of a coral reef, through which a sand shark nosed with an inquisitive expression. A place to eat fish? We sat at the outdoor tables and marveled at tanks of lobsters which pranced about in slow motion, exploring with their feelers the hopeless possibility of escape. Farther inside the cul-de-sac stood temples and waterfalls, a whole miniature landscape of Thai spires, model swans, palanquins, glass cockerels, and carefully cut trees. This was *sanuk* instead of architecture, or *sanuk* as architecture, and it was like being inside a department store where all the departments have been thrown together. "I call it life-giving tack," McGinnis said. "Soul candy."

With its Kloster signs and gimcrack awnings, the market was a working-class place, big tables of bawling eaters hot with endless plates of *hor mor* and *tom yum*, each table accompanied by a metal tray with an ice bucket. The waitresses wore black ties and short skirts. At the end of the strip stood a replica of a temple with a line of stone elephants. The lamps were held up by gold garudas, their sex appeal heightened by a few sacrilegious curves, and among them sparkled the glass cockerels, gratuitous things that caused the groups of ice-cream-eating adolescents in white socks to pause. I thought, "Middle-aged men also love this sort of tack," and before I knew it I was happy again, with the happiness of belonging to a crowd of families, with their small children racing about and the air filled with balloons. This outdoor terrace was framed by corroded eaves and trellises of leaves, and next to it boomed a nightclub with the usual toga-wearing hostesses. But there was no separation between this adult sphere and the family one. The two belonged to each other, paid no attention to each other, and merged with mutual confidence.

When I thought about the men I knew here, I considered their world to be one-dimensional because women were not a part of it, not on the deepest level. It was a world of men alone. And if the claim that a man unmarried is only half a man is true (Dr. Johnson), then they were half-men, semi-men without fullness in their emotional life. Rag dolls on the loose.

But at the same time, I didn't factor in this side of their experience, this other happiness which came only in passing moments. It arose as the result of a free coming and going, a sweet immersion in the life of a large city. They moved around as they liked, and in that respect they were surprisingly lordly. They didn't obey the laws of economic gravity.

McGinnis talked about his wife, but after a while I began to feel that he didn't really have one, that it was just another invention and that the next time I saw him she would have disappeared. I looked down at his peeling sandals and the frayed hems, and it could have been that he was not really working either, that he was moonlighting and part-timing, and that he was writing (as he often claimed) in his spare time. He had brought me to the White House, he said, because he was going dancing with some friends of his at a club nearby called Pump Up.

"I know what you're thinking," he said slyly. "No, it's not a gay club."

I said I didn't care if it was a gay club. I rather liked gay clubs.

"I have been thinking," he said, "how odd it is to see you here again. You seem to be going back and forth. You're in the back-and-forth phase. I went back and forth for years before I settled down here. By the time I settled down, I had been back and forth so much that the place seemed completely familiar to me. It was like losing one skin and acquiring another, or crossing from one side of a river to the other. You go back and forth between East and West and pretty soon you have no idea who the fuck you are anymore. You could say that it's a problem typical of the contemporary condition, and it's all because of airplanes. Without airplanes we wouldn't be in this predicament. The age of spending all one's life in one shitty country or one shitty city is over."

"But what about your wife?"

"Have you ever observed how a married man, when he lives in a large city with plenty of social opportunities, almost never spends his nights at home? He wanders about, he's even more nomadic that the single guy. He's even more *single* than the single guy. All it takes is fifteen years of conjugal bliss. Life is the hearth, and life is movement. The two can't be reconciled."

"But look around you. Families everywhere having a good time."

"No, *you* look around you. What's that you see across the street there? Oh, a five-storey massage parlor! That's what Asian family life is predicated on. No divorce, and massage parlors everywhere."

It was an easy walk to Pump Up. It stood at the edge of an open space which must have been cleared by bulldozers, for the tenements all around pressed in. At the entrance to the complex stood a multistorey spirit house painted dark red, inside which sat a model couple primly listening to the hip-hop pounding from the Hip Zone Happiness Club. We walked across the parking lot shadowed by cranes and went first into the Super Performance Club.

We sat near a window under buildings draped with green netting. "Isn't this great?" McGinnis kept saying, but I wasn't sure that either of us thought it was great. I wasn't sure either of us wouldn't have been happier at that moment sitting under an oak tree in Tuscany with a glass of chianti. But we weren't in Tuscany and never would be because we were broke bastards, and broke bastards don't get a look-in when it comes to the hills of Siena.

"We are rather lucky in a way," he said with curious feeling, and half getting up, so that he looked like a tall, near-extinct bird about to launch into flight. His arms even opened out like two atrophied wings and made their first flap. "And you are a fool to be leaving. Waiter, two Cambodian brandies!"

The waiters explained that Cambodian brandy didn't exist, at least not in Bangkok discos, and his reply to them was, "But I had it last time!" So they brought us schnapps on a tray instead, and McGinnis was happy to turn them into a toast, and then another. They were playing Tommy James and the Shondells—a nostalgia night—and was it "Crimson and Clover"? Before long a Thai acquaintance of McGinnis came up, a beautiful boy with the famed family name of Bunnag, and we took some coke lined on the back of a lacquer box. I hadn't done coke in years, and its effect was enhanced by this long period of estrangement. I went to dance with the boy and his girlfriends, and before I had realized it McGinnis had slipped away: I wouldn't see him again for two years, and I understood that this was his way of operating, that he came and went according to moods of sadness, embarrassment, and regret. He was a strange man, and a fugitive one, like one of those lost uncles which every family has, a man who shows up for three days at Christmas to pull crackers and play the piano and never at any other time, whose life no one knows anything about and whose activities are always suspect and distant, unconnected to family values. But on the spur of the moment it was easy to forget how appalling this was. One of the girls was called On, and she took me for a ride along Rama IV on her motorbike, high on her expensive coke, and I was sure that at one point we were alone in a small park of wet trees and I could hear barges tooting down the river and we were dancing barefoot to music that didn't exist—or was it a room with orange curtains, and was the dance another numberless act of love?

THE SUPRAGLOTTAL STRUCTURES

Two years went by. And then one night, as if those years had suddenly flattened into a few minutes, I arrived back in Bangkok as if I had never left. I took a car from the airport to Sukhumvit Soi 51 near Thong Lor, where I had rented a small cottage for the year, and I realized that yet again it was Christmas, and I always seemed to be here at Christmas. The house lay within a larger property owned by a member of the Thai aristocracy connected to the royal family, and by the metal gates a groundsman stood with a flashlight, waiting for me, in the light-cappuccino uniform of a South American traffic cop. The staff came out to see me, maids, gardeners, children. He opened the door for me, and at once a dozen dogs behind the gates began barking. Kitty, the mistress of the house, he explained in a hushed voice, collected them off the streets as a charitable hobby.

We stepped into a garden with jungle trees, and up to a wire fence where the diseased hounds came limping and snarling. We went past them down a lawn from which tiny frogs burst out around our feet like heated popcorn. The cottage at the garden's end was made almost entirely of glass, its main room sitting like a three-sided showroom among the trees. The family estate contained old warehouses which screened the cottage's back garden, where an imposing mango tree grew. Even at night, one of the gardeners was pruning it. He came over with a machete, doffing his straw hat, and helped with the bags.

"Is Miss Kitty still up?"

"Yes, sir. She is making drinks."

The main windows of the house were lit, and through them appeared rooms of antique furniture, ceramic lamps, and beveled mirrors. At the other end of the garden, a spirit house came to life, the candles lit by the staff. The rain stopped.

I noticed now that the entire household staff were standing around the pool, their hands crossed before them. Priscilla, the head maid, turned on the toadstool lamps behind the ponds and an Angkorian statue emerged out of the dark. The house had sweeping traditional eaves, bringers of shade by day and shadow by night. Candles were lit along the paths, and the gardener said to me, "Sawasdee krap," taking off his hat again. Cicadas rasped in the mango trees, competing with the Phyloglossus frogs, and frangipani petals rained down onto the pool.

Soon I saw Kitty dancing with a man in the main windows. To my surprise, she was young and chic and her laughter carried through plate glass. But as I slept that night, something happened to shatter the comfortable mood that had immediately taken hold of me. I was woken by a sore throat, and soon there was a fever, the throat gradually worsening and saliva pouring out of my mouth. Lying on my side, I watched the stars above the walls and found myself counting for no reason, like a child who counts to a hundred to see if his toothache will end. But within an hour my windpipe began to close and I could no longer breathe. I ran down Soi 51 to the main road in shorts, unable to breathe, flagging down a cab with a terrible finger. The last word I spoke for a week was *roong-pa-yaa-baan*—hospital.

•

Most foreigners go to Bumrungrad, the largest private hospital in Asia, on Sukhumvit Soi 1. Half resort, half luxury hospital, Bumrungrad has earned fame in a number of medical
areas, notably plastic surgery and heart operations. It is the
largest sex-change facility in the world. Westerners flock
there, not only to change their sex but also to have babies, to undergo dermal procedures and hair transplants.
Soon they'll be going there to die as well, because it's far
cheaper.

It was a Saturday morning and the emergency rooms
were empty. I was taken to Ear, Nose, and Throat, where a
young Thai doctor took my blood pressure and examined
the inflamed throat. Looking at the thermometer, his brow
contracted with that expression of controlled consternation
of which doctors are the masters.

"It's not a sore throat," he said gently. "It's worse. It
may have something to do with the supraglottal structures."

It was an infection possibly carried by particles of dust,
Dr. Somnath theorized, particles coated with pathogens to
which my immune system had no resistance. To get a clear
picture, a fiber-optic camera would have to be passed via the
nose and into the throat itself. The nurse prepared a gurney.
As this was done, a calmant was administered to me, and,
feeling happier than I usually do, I recalled the words that
Krishna addresses to Arjuna on the battlefield of Kuru in the
Bhaghavad Gita (I keep it always by my side, though not
during this particular ordeal): Pleasure and pain, he says, are
transient. They come and go. "A particle of dust inhaled on
the street," the doctor went on, "something eaten at a mar-

ket, a gulp of swimming pool water, a mango even—all these are possible culprits in the inflaming of the epiglottis.

"I am afraid that you will not be able to leave the hospital for at least ten days. We will have to get you on to an antihistamine drip within an hour: if the inflammation doesn't subside, we shall have to puncture your throat to get the air in and out, and perhaps even your lungs. Did you know that the father of your nation, George Washington, died of it?"

•

Old age and death are constantly on our minds. What will they be like? Will Arjuna's advice be of any use? There is nothing about drooling in the Bhavagad Gita. I arrived at the Reservations Desk, which was like that of a hotel, and was given a menu of rooms. The medical consumer is presented with a menu of room options in a bound folder, with the prices and amenities laid out with the utmost simplicity. The De Luxe Suites seemed the best option for 4,000 baht a night, since one gets a desk, a private lounge area, sofas, and entertainment options, along with sunnier views from high up in the "residential" tower. Unfortunately, they were all booked. Next down the ladder, however, were the smaller two-room De Luxe Suites. At 3,000 baht there were also the Luxury Single Rooms. And then there were the Double Units, shared with another patient, with a shared bathroom.

We moved through corridors filled with invalids, many Arabs in keffiyeh, Iranian women with canes, Chinese millionaires with families in tow, all of them with the look of people who are simultaneously stricken and pampered. An international city of the wounded. Strapped to the gurney, there were only moments to count before I was on the seventh floor, being undressed by the nurses. The seventh floor was populated by Thais and by the occasional wealthy *farang*, expats who obviously came here on a regular basis. The hospital as cheap diversion, a vacation within a vacation. There was a large lounge area with children's toys, international business magazines, and televisions. Potted plants made it look more like an upscale clinic.

After I had been dressed in minuscule pajamas with an elephant motif, three intravenous drips were connected to my wrist, the little plastic gauges and taps tightened, the drips adjusted. The nurses washed my hands, and they are nurses unlike any others: slender and in stiff bonnets decorated with a single navy line. They alone are able to puncture a vein flirtatiously; and they do so flawlessly, drawing off a little blood in the buffer and then adjusting the three separate tubes inside an adhesive bandage.

Through the window on the far side of the curtain came a truncated snapshot of a neighborhood such as one could see anywhere in this metropolis: wilted palms pecked by birds, roof gardens laid out at surprising angles, AC units stacked along back walls, a maid arranging a room of French furniture. A city like many others near the equator, neither more nor less peeling or blistered or shamed.

Sometime in the depth of that night the light of the corridor fell into the room and a girl in stiletto heels and a black cocktail dress slipped into the room with a careful stealth, making herself as quiet as possible, and with a bouquet of white roses and a boxed cake of some kind she darted into the far side of the partition with rustles and scent and threw herself into the other man's arms, tussling, unwrapping, encouraging. I heard the distinct pop of buttons being undone in practiced haste. A tryst, an encounter—which was surely illegal according to hospital rules?

I was going to press the emergency bell, but I was then stirred by a calm curiosity, because the patient was sighing, "Mimi, Mimi," with a pitiful intensity and I decided to listen and say nothing. An ancient sound, you could say. They laughed and rolled around. The flowers fell on the floor, and under the curtain appeared a single dyed-blue rose in aluminum wrapping, which lay there all night. So I began to construct a mental picture of this improvident satyr. They whispered through a thunderstorm, and as I lay wide awake, alert to the smallest sexual sound, I looked over and noticed the impressively serious books on his night table. A volume of Heine; Bizot's classic account of Cambodia under Pol Pot, *The Gate*; and some contemporary German novels whose authors I had never heard of. Confined with a stranger in a hospital ward and afflicted by an illness I had never heard of, I rushed to hate this man, whose name was Fritzy. His girl murmured it over and over. Looking behind the curtain, I saw her placing slices of banana between his lips. It was at this moment that the nurses came in to take our blood pressure, and now, surely, I'd have my revenge. But not at all. They merely apologized to the happy couple for interrupting their pleasures. With me they were more severe, and they assumed I could not understand Thai.

"He looks half dead."

"Does he have any relatives in Bangkok?"

"I think he's a tourist. They always die alone."

I was able to pull the curtain aside and see Fritzy's identification label dangling from his drip tree, which read *Herr Friedrich Furnau, Blood Type A*. Mimi left at first light, without a sound, and I came out of a nightmare to glimpse Fritzy making his way to the bathroom.

•

Without turning on a light, he shuffled in his regulation slippers to the bathroom, where for a moment he shot me a look, and then a wink. I remembered an entry that Samuel Pepys made in his diary in which he describes being caught by his wife in the act of "touzing" her companion Deb Willet, about which he remarks, "I was certainly deep in her cunny and at a wondrous loss for words to explain it." So, Fritzy, I thought as if speaking to him directly, are you at a wondrous loss for words to explain it?

He came out of the bathroom and I saw now that there was something Neanderthal about him, with his extended arms, his hairy back, and his squat face, which all contributed to a look of prehistory, of virile primitivity which was quite startling. His swollen blue eyes sought me out and there was a distant, sad look in them that was arresting in its way. Mimi and Fritzy. What kind of life was it?

•

"I should tell you something about epiglottitis," Somnath said later as he sat by my bed, with that conciliatory spirit that Thai doctors so often manage to project in the midst of life's horrors, acting as if horrors themselves were necessary entertainments which could be enjoyed at a distance. He showed me a colored illustration of the human throat in which the leaf-shaped epiglottis coated with mucous membrane was clearly marked. The nasopharyngoscopy they had done had also yielded some alarming images. The risk of death was high, Somnath went on, because of the difficulty in intubating patients with extensive swelling of the supraglottal structures. The airways become obstructed quickly, and basically—well, he smiled, you strangle to death in about an hour. In extremis, they could puncture the trachea, but it didn't always work. One more day alone in my house, he said, and I would have been dead. Onset and progression of symptoms were remarkably rapid, and to make things absolutely clear, he then went through those symptoms one by one, as if I needed to understand them properly. Sore throat, odynophagia or dysphagia (muffled voice), drooling (inability to handle secretions), cervical adenopathy, tripod position (sitting up on the hands, with the tongue out and head forward), hypoxia, fever, stridor (advanced airway obstruction), respiratory distress, tachycardia, irritability, and, best of all, "toxic appearance of patient."

I could tell that Fritzy was listening carefully to all this.

Pharyngeal cultures taken from people with acute epiglottitis frequently yield a wide range of pathogens, which include the following: *Eschericihia coli*, *Fusobacterium necrophorum*, *Klebsiella pneumoniae*, *Enterobacter cloacae*, Group A Streptococci, herpes simplex virus, infectious mononucleosis, and Aspergillus.

"Of course," Somnath added, suddenly standing still and sending himself deep into parallel thoughts, "I cannot rule out a *Bacteroides melanogenicus.*"

•

During that second night, my fever raged. From down the corridor came the chanting of Buddhist monks at a deathbed, the smell of sad incense and a whiff of Dettol. At the ends of these corridors the dead were memorialized by small shrines with photographs and flowers, and anyone who died during the night in Bumrungrad could end up as a shrine photo.

I thought even more seriously about death and cremation. Then a hand swept aside the plastic curtain and the head on the far side stared directly at me with those sad, immoveable eyes. Fritzy pointed to his throat and said, "So you got it in the throat, did you?"

There lay the notepad on the night table between us, and I decided to write a reply.

Got what?

"Got it," he repeated. "You got it in the throat."

Epiglottitis.

"Epiglottitis in the throat?"

Where else?

He looked at me seriously, then turned the TV off. We

lay in the dark, the red glare of the city bathed us, and he said, "Isn't that life-threatening?"

And when I said it was, he nodded, as if he knew exactly what this might mean for all concerned.

"I gave myself a Thai name," he went on irrelevantly, and he pointed to the name tag on his drips. Now that I looked at it again, it read *Thatsit* as well as *Fritzy*. Herr Thatsit Furnau.

•

Fritzy was watching live fly-fishing on Sky TV. He imitated the looping throws of these competing and notable anglers with his right hand, which reared up and back, then flicked into space as if hurling a plastic dragonfly into the dark waters of a Scottish stream. "*Ay*," he said from time to time, echoing the expressions of these competitors, who are men of few words. However, he said not a word to me throughout four hours of live angling, and I wondered if he, like all viewers of live angling, had entered a parallel mental universe, shaped itself like a shallow stream which drowned out all thought. But in the middle of the afternoon of that second day, the nurses came in and I heard a subdued struggle on the far side of the curtain. "Leave it alone—" the German snapped.

"Mr. Furnau, it's your injection."

"Fuck my injection. I want my lawyer!"

A syringe was brought into the room and there was a quiet sobbing. I gripped the edges of the bed. To die in a white room, among smiling angels—in Room 7036. And I thought of the earl of Rochester murmuring to his penis: *Tell, my prick, can this be death?* A specialist appeared in a tweedy suit. The discussion rattled on under the strip lights which made everything look blue and metallic; the pictures of windmills in Greece, the bowls of tweezers and swabs, the iodine bottles. The specialist spoke in Wall Street School English.

"Mr. Furnau, the infection has spread. One in every one hundred and seventy cases. The swelling has not gone down as we had hoped. One moment, please. Now, let me explain. We must go ahead with a third injection, and probably we operate tomorrow morning."

"You can't save it?"

The specialist tried to make a joke out of it, as specialists often do, because they can afford to.

"Sperm count," he whispered, "remains exactly the same! Exactly. You can have more children, Mr. Thatsit Furnau."

"Thatsit Furnau," the German echoed.

The doctors left and we were alone again. I reached for a small bottle of Lucozade that I had ordered from room service and forced it down. Surprisingly, it opened up my throat a little and for the first time in two days I felt as if I could utter a word or two. I lay back and watched the bubbles flowing down the plastic tubes toward the buffer, slow but regular like the workings of a klepshydra, and it reminded me that my body, too, was a clock of sorts, and it would run down eventually. Fritzy then put down the magazine he was reading and asked, "Are you awake?"

He picked up the nurse bell and pressed it. The sweetest of our nurses, Lila, appeared, and he said, "Lila, can we have two champagnes, please?"

I tried to laugh, but she simply replied, "One minute," and after that minute had expired the champagne arrived.

"This," Fritzy said, "is what I love about Thailand. You ask for two glasses of champagne in a hospital, and they give it to you."

"But," Lila objected, "Miss Lalant can *no have*."

I looked at the tag on my drip: I was marked as *Miss Lalant*.

"Miss Lalant," Fritzy said, "can have the champagne put into his intravenous tube. It is *farang* custom."

"Oh? No you joke me."

"No joke. I'm serious."

The invalid thinks constantly of life outside the hospital. He is now an outsider to normal existence, and therefore the inside of his room acquires a critical mass. He notices both the minute details of its furniture—every nut and bolt, every brand name on the clocks and medical instruments—and the city's electricity, which seeps through the windows. The outer world seems even more glamorous now. Street corners with sports bars and bamboo-screen eateries, and girls in miniskirts sitting on stools bigger than them, sipping at coconuts out of straws. The Land of Sanuk-Dukkha. It was just there, at the end of a driveway, but frustratingly distant because it was located at the far end of a sickness. Fritzy and I both thought of it with longing: the heat like a Mississippi swamp, the animal swagger and the smell of mango skins piling in the gutters, the sweetness of decay that stirs the penis to life, just at the insolent tip.

Portofino Trattoria on the first floor lacked only a mulberry tree and a few sickles on the walls to make it something fully blown in that style that could be called Italian Rustic, but it did have trompe l'oeil murals with little views of the Coliseum circa 1780 and reconstructions of the Roman Forum. It is enough, is it not? And there was a long bar behind which stood the confused mural Dennis had once spoken of, highlighting a row of bottles. Helix's mural, I thought suddenly. But that must have been a tall tale.

Fritzy and I went in, maneuvering our drips through the doors, which were held open for us by charming waitresses. It would be an arresting sight in a Western hospital, but not here, for the place is actually full of people with drips. A man sits with a drip at his side as the wine list is opened for him, a napkin tucked into his pajamas. We went to the bar, which was better stocked than many bars in New York nightclubs, with a line of aged scotches, curaçaos, and designer vodkas.

Fritzy was a familiar here, and there was a braggadocio to his limp, a braggadocio that didn't quite work, not even here. A dying man blustering his way into a pub full of cronies. The bar was in fact filled with crippled and invalid *farang*s in varying degrees of decrepitude. Wrapped in bandages and splints, they sat smoking in front of Camparis, gazing at the mural of Christ at a drinking party of Alexander the Great. Wasn't that Saint Peter swigging a bottle of Gordon's?

It was like a bar in a Sicilian village, a camaraderie of old men who do nothing but talk, because every other avenue of life has been closed off. The look in the eyes is intensely distant, expressing a constant reckoning with medical fate. They were mostly British, with a few Germans and French among them, and all of them looked the worse for wear. One said, "Wotcha, Fritz," and winked as Fritzy glided past. They brushed knuckles, like gangsters.

We sat at the bar's end and the waitress asked if we were permitted to drink.

"Absolutely."

No further questions were asked.

"Two glasses of champagne, Jill."

Under the red lanterns of the Ayame sushi restaurant next door, a girl in a kimono stood in white socks, bowing between two curtains decorated with fish. Fritzy got us a table close to the windows, so we could people-watch. Bumrungrad has a true *passeggiata* every night and the Middle Eastern patients in particular take to the "streets" en masse, circulating through the corridors of the all-night malls in their best clothes.

Women on crutches with face masks flirted openly with men suffering from epileptic fits and sciatica. Hobbling, limping, squinting, this injured mass proved that the sex drive is the supreme of all instincts and cannot be suppressed even by terminal cancer. We lust till we die, we concluded with some relief, and ordered Tuscan white bean soup. "A straw for the gentleman," Fritzy asked the waiter, and we watched the *passeggiata*. I noticed that his right hand was limp, and shook a little. "As happier men watch birds," Evelyn Waugh wrote, "I watch men." I was delighted by the ease with which the straw was provided, as if it were no more unusual than a soup spoon, and the delicacy with which our drips were treated by the servers who danced around us. An invalid restaurant where you could smoke and drink and suck Tuscan white bean soup through a straw. Everything is commonsense and in proportion.

"This," Fritzy said, "is why Thailand is the best country to get sick and die in, in spite of the obvious vileness of all doctors. You can actually half-enjoy your demise. You can enjoy the *service*."

I could now talk in a hoarse whisper, so I was able to say, "You sound like you intend to die here."

"I do intend to die here. What? Am I supposed to die in Deutschland?"

Gruffly, he savaged open a pack of Alain Delon, Cambodian cigarettes.

"Look at that." He smiled. "The Cambodians call their cigarettes Alain fucking Delon. Some genius must've thought that one up."

"The Alain Delons will hasten it."

"What? You mean dying? Jesus. Don't you think I have enough problems without worrying about my lungs and Alain Delons? They're going to give me a ballectomy. That's right, they going to cut out the left ball. Even my lawyer can't stop them. You'd think we had some legal right over our own balls, but no. They are very cavalier, I must say, with other people's privata."

"Privata?"

"It's a word, it's a word—our private particulars. They lop them off on a moment's notice, *woosh*."

"But isn't it to save your life?"

"As if you have a life without a ball. I'm telling you, they enjoy it. It's pure sadism. Doctors. Nurses. The lot of them. Lawyers. Especially lawyers. Lawyers love watching you having your left testicle removed. For them it's a metaphor for what they do all the time."

He shot down his Australian bubbly and lit up. Could you really smoke in a hospital restaurant?

"How is your blood pressure?"

"No idea."

"Jill, two vodka tonics please."

He was a real German, relaxed, permissive, blue-eyed. But behind his cragged face and lopsided gentlemanly smile lay a darkness of soul. It's an appealing combination if you're not on the receiving end of the darkness of soul. Germans loved Thailand, but in a different way from the British. They were more cynical about themselves, and therefore less cynical about the Thais, the very reverse of the British mentality. They settled down often, married, happily took on the onerous burden of supporting an extended family in the girl's home village up in Issan. They were fatalistic, and being fatalistic was a good trait to have in a fatalistic country like Thailand. Except when it came to losing a ball.

"The insurance," he growled, grasping at one of the Alain Delons and sucking on it like a straw. "They have a value scale for different parts of the body. Three thousand euros for the ball."

"Each?"

"Of course each. Six thousand for the whole package, if you are so unlucky. But, get this, five thousand for a foot. Ten thousand for an arm. A million for the head, ha ha. I asked them if I could switch the arm for the ball, because, you know, the ball is much more important to me than the arm. And it's seven thousand more. I could build a garage next to my house in Pattaya for that. But of course the problem isn't in my arm. It's in my inner tubes. Reverse infection or something. Men in their fifties. What a life. *Verdammt.*"

His voice got louder the more he ranted, and his eyes became pale and delicate as cornflowers threatened by a combine harvester.

A drink, an Alain Delon, a hospitable ear—the invalid doesn't need much. Fritzy cast an appreciative eye over the mural in front of us and his brow tensed. Alexander or Christ, one couldn't decide.

"If you had a choice between the ball and your head?" I asked.

"I'd keep the ball, obviously. A million! I could build a house in Ko Samui."

Finally, I asked him what he did for a living. Even in Thailand you have to have a living.

"I run a Mercedes dealership in Pattaya. Oh yes, and I also have a small hotel on the beach. It's sort of a *boum-boum* hotel, but aren't they all? We do have families stay there as well. We're popular with holidaymakers from the Pfalz. Word has gotten out there that we are good value. Sunshine Hotel." He leaned over and there was a whiff of fennel seeds on his teeth. "We have a disco for the under-tens. Beanbags."

That night, we lay in bed, playing cards. Down the hall, a choir with handbells sang Christmas carols and people in the neighboring rooms sang along. What day was it? The 20th? The 21st? The nurses took our blood pressure a little before midnight and refilled the drips. One always has the feeling that they are privy to a secret concerning the immediate future. We drifted in and out of a heavy sleep imposed by the sedatives, and when I was half-awake I was sure that I could hear someone padding up and down the corridor in socks.

"It's the ghost," came Fritzy's voice in the dark. "It's the old woman who died in this room last month."

•

Ghosts, in Thai, are called *phi*. There are innumerable kinds. There are *phi pop*, evil ghosts, or *phi kraseu*, often portrayed as a woman with a head made of intestines. There are spirits called *phi am* which sit on a person's chest and make breathing difficult: in the northeast part of the country it's believed that these are the ghosts of widows, and men paint their mouths with lipstick before going to bed so that the widow spirits will think they are women and leave them alone. The ghosts of people who died violently are called *phi tai hong*. After the 2004 tsunami, there were hundreds of sightings of these near the country's beaches. Many rural Thais believe that simply walking about at night puts one within grasp of these ghosts.

But not all ghosts are entirely fearful. I would soon discover that my house on Soi 51 was also haunted, by the ghosts of Kitty's uncle and aunt. The staff claimed unhesitatingly that they saw them pottering about the garden, inspecting the mango trees. But when aunt and uncle crossed the lawns at midnight there was no sense of alarm. Quite the contrary. Such things were related with a shrug in the voice, and the servants would say things like, "If you come out here, sir, you'll see them too. They are sometimes carrying a tea kettle. They inspect the mango trees to see that we're pruning them properly."

•

Fritzy and I then took to daily promenades around the hospital in our pajamas. We looked like a couple of crime bosses from *Oliver Twist*, picking our way through the consumer outlets which we couldn't patronize, people-watching at the ground-floor Starbucks. Eventually we found a way to sneak outside, and so down a side street to Soi 1. After five days and nights of continuous air-conditioning, the heat took me by surprise and we moved slowly, but unremarked by the crowds, as if invalids from Bumrungrad often used this escape route. Where were we to stop—Bunny Bar? Bamboo Bar? Tahiti Bar? The bars of Soi 1 are tolerant of hospital uniforms, of the general messiness of the sick, and the girls mobbed us. Sick men, sick men! Down Soi 1 came the sound of "We Wish You a Merry Christmas," sung at breakneck speed in contralto, and I suddenly felt happy again, reunited with the sound of ice in a tilted gin and tonic. Moreover, Fritzy's eyes were green as primitive ferns, but unlike those graceful plants they also slopped from side to side like loose water in a bucket. I had no idea who this man was, or why he was spending time with me. I surmised that he was bored, that his medications had gone to his head, as mine had to mine.

"This is my last night of having two testicles. I think a toast is in order. Farewell to youth and all that. From now on, I will be half-castrated. My ex-wife will be very happy."

"Are you going back to Pattaya?"

He ignored me. "Night on Soi 1! Marvelous. Shall we go to a girly bar? We're only ten minutes from Nana."

"With drips?"

"What difference do drips make? When is a man not up for a girly bar?"

"When he is connected to an IV drip."

"My left ball is aching for one last adventure. Can we not take him on a last farewell visit to a girly bar?"

The Nana Complex doesn't get busy until after ten, but even then the twenty-odd bars were up and rolling. We went into Rainbow II, on the second floor, where the dance platforms were already full, and sat at a bench with two Singhas. Fritzy was pale and uncertain-looking, his mouth quivering slightly as he sipped at his bottle. It was a ritual more than an active pleasure spiced by novelty. But, personally, what I have always enjoyed in the bars of Nana and Soi Cowboy (I exempt the hideous tourist traps of Patpong) is the lack of menacing bouncers, the calm and relaxed ordinariness of the show. No men, in other words, except the humble clients, who are not there to make trouble. If one insists, one can laugh at the whole charade, or sneer at it. It's up to you. But I've never seen any need to do either. The show itself consists of girls dancing around poles, and by law they are now required to wear bikinis. On average, they dance quite badly, but there is a lot of giggling and horseplay, and the girls who are waiting for their set sit around with the clients, teasing the girls who are on. There are times when they get into a groove. If a *luuk thung* hit comes on, the northern girls from Issan all get up and start dancing and singing on the tables, suddenly nostalgic. If they pick up a client, they go downstairs with him and make an offering at the Ganesha shrine near the exit. The elephant god receives their gift and grants them credit. What characterizes this entire operation is the absence of any atmosphere of brimstone or anger, its clumsy naïveté and lack of self-consciousness, or at least a self-consciousness which has not yet toppled over into *sin*.

Fritzy drank beer after beer and I tried to slow him down.

"What I like," he said, "is the way these places make you feel like the planet is spinning round and round and nothing matters. It's all a sham and it will all disappear quickly, much quicker than we think. It's just a bit of amusement before we nod off forever. It's not a place for the young. And what do they know, anyway? It's a place for the dying. Only the dying—in flesh or in spirit—can grasp how pretty it really is. These places are all about death. It's like bodybuilding or health crazes, only it's more living. We come here, we get a hard-on, and we feel the dying speeding up. But it makes us smile at least. No? It makes us see around life's corners. So drink up, Miss Lalant, and death to all those who think they are superior to us!"

In the large Erawan shrine on the hospital grounds, meanwhile, stood dozens of elephant statues, pachyderms which are thought to bring good luck to the sick. And in homage to this idea relatives of patients knelt in prayer before them, buried in a mushroom of incense smoke. The shrine seemed odd so close to the hospital, odd in its seriousness, but the onlooker is suddenly touched by that crowd of model elephants, some tiny, some quite large. Long ago, the intangible qualities of elephants had touched people and induced them to transfer to the elephants the idea of a god who could dispense compassion. It was a subtle observation about elephants, and it was an Asian feeling, but not ours, alas. Here, the streets teem with animals. Elephants wander down them, with rear-end lights attached to their tails; monkeys scatter through trees.

•

My last night at Bumrungrad was not the fête I had hoped for, since Fritzy had not reappeared. My tubes were disconnected and I read the horoscopes in a pile of women's magazines I had bought in the lobby. I noticed then that Fritzy had left his card for me on my night table. It bore the name of his hotel and car dealership in Pattaya, and he had scrawled on the back, "Visit me when you're well."

I arrived downstairs the next day in my clothes, which had been freshly laundered and pressed: the recently released patient often appears as a prisoner collecting his valuables from a prison safe-box after a moderate incarceration. It was ninety-one in the shade, and the sunlight had an antiseptic, stinging edge. A smell of mint and cooking oil heated with chilies wafted down the street, rotting guava, the joys of the gutters which are always overflowing, and a whiff of camphor from a passing inmate. The hospital flags flew proudly above Bumrungrad's monumental gates. "International Man," they seemed to cry, "come here for your epiglottitis!"

I stepped into the sun, basked for a moment by the elephant shrine, where I lit a joss stick for Fritzy, then one of the boys in white naval uniforms saluted and flagged me a cab. He asked me where I was going.

"Sukhumvit Road," I said. "Soi 51."

The boy leaned down to the window. *Sukhumvit haa sip ek.*

After the words for throat, blood, pee, blood test, pineapple, and boredom, this was almost the first complete Thai phrase I ever repeated in my sleep. Even later, when I had forgotten why I came here at all and how I ever managed to leave, the words had a mystic comfort, the sonority of something like "home." Barely half an hour later I was at the corner of Soi 51, and, surprisingly, it looked unfamiliar, though I couldn't say why, and equally enigmatically I had the certain feeling that Fritzy was dead.

After an illness the body takes its time. It is usually a period of great peace and clarity, sleep alternating with reading and swimming, the sun working its cure day by day. I spent Christmas alone, and then on Boxing Day went up to the house for one of Kitty's High Society parties, where I cut a thin and wasted figure among the tuxedos and tans. I was lost in every sense, but Kitty sought me out, and she surprised me with her plum British accent, fruit of a Somerset boarding school, and her free and easy attitude toward men. It is constantly remarked that the Thais are rather formal and proper in their day-to-day lives, a conservatism summed up in the phrase *rab rioy*. But it could be said that it is this very surface reticence which frees the deeper, more private self to be sexually anarchic. In this respect, one might venture to add, they are the inverse of Americans and Britishers, who are so often flaunting their supposed freedom in your face but who are invariably easy to offend. It is the tension between the calm, reticent surface and the adventurous core which arouses me more than the reverse.

"Sick?" Kitty said at once. "The maid said you had cancer. Or you had found a girl. Every foreign man finds a girl in three seconds."

I liked her more and more, though there was a bold, pushy side to her, and she didn't hesitate to be tactile. The Thai upper class are a strange world unto themselves, but they do not suffer from the nervous fragility of an elite living in a run-down country where revolution is a constant possibility. Quite the reverse. The elite here is Westernized, Anglophone, confident in itself and in Asia. It actively revels in flashy cars, designer rags, and Banyan Tree weekends. Kitty's own garage was stocked with BMW convertibles, Jeeps, and sundry town cars, and she went every day to a California gym in one of the shopping malls on nearby Thong Lor. Her friends were of the same class, with foreigners added like spice to a routine meal, and they danced around the pool to Bone Thugs-N-Harmony before heading out to a bar on Silom.

I wasn't sure of my step with them. There was a feeling that we belonged to the same class. But if anyone had asked what that class was I couldn't have said. I never yearned to mingle with them, since belonging to a class is always accidental except for the industrious social climber.

•

At the corner of Soi 51, across from the twenty-four-hour Cal Tex station and the Chavala Turkish Bath, stands a green sign with an arrow: *The Wells International School*. A mass of dangling cables hangs over the intersection, and above them looms a neon sign which spells *Yuasa Battery*. Across from this sign, in turn, red and blue neons delineate the word *Chavala* in Thai and English over leafy shadows on Soi 34. It's a massage parlor built in 1959 where the bathwater is reputedly brown and the corridors haunted by the souls of clients past. From now on, it will be my most familiar street corner, the place I pass every day, a hundred times a day.

The Yuasa sign on the corner stands above a store called Spa and Pool, in the window of which can be seen the surprising internal organs of Jacuzzis. Thus the corner is dominated by the signs of Cal Tex, Yuasa, Chavala, and Spa and Pool: a compendium of human needs. Fuel, electricity, sex. A half-naked man sometimes stands gibbering by the Jacuzzi machines, his matted hair falling to his chest like that of a deranged holy man. A policeman has descended from his motorcycle in his shiny boots and is walking across to him. The scene is turning ominous.

•

Just behind this junction with Sukhumvit stands a cluster of Japanese entertainment venues destined exclusively for the thousands of Tokyo salarymen who populate this neighborhood. To the left there is a sushi bar with outdoor table and slanted crates of ice holding chilled sprats, sea cucumbers, snails. Next to it is a karaoke bar with tinted windows. And across the road is a more grandiose hostess bar on the ground floor of a *satai roman* mansion, with a sign that reads *Japanese*, in English, as if to warn off all others, and a pair of glass doors that reveal five or six beauties in red evening gowns filling out a rococo boudoir.

The *soi* runs past all this. Behind the walls lie the mansions of the Thai rich, gardens shrilling with cicadas, scrolled iron gates with gilding, spirit houses raised on pedestals so high they can be seen from the street, twinkling with fairylights and cheap candles. There is the Wells School: a British teacher doing gymnastics with a crowd of Thai girls shouting in British accents.

When I had recovered my balance, I went with a walking

stick and a thick hat along this path next to the Wells School
and came out at the Thong Lor Skytrain station. This section of Sukhumvit is suddenly enclosed in claustrophobic
shadow, the sun blotted out as tenements crowd around the
Skytrain structures, offering defunct signs for language
schools and dentists. There is a model-car store at the corner
called Tifosi filled with little Ferraris, and across the road the
employees of Cal Tex stand with red flags, waving down
motorists. They erupt into chants, and dance.

At the corner of Thong Lor the pineapple sellers are
always massed under the Skytrain columns, where the shade
is darkest. The cry goes up: *Sapporot!* There is the old man
playing the *khaen* bamboo pipes, making his weird atonal
noises. I stopped by the lines of lottery tickets and tabloids
laid out along the sidewalks, breathed in the bowls of *yen ta
foh* and the boxes of sweet tamarinds looking like small
blood sausages. I looked into the lobby of the Gunn's
"apartment block for ladies" by the Thong Lor station—
for what?—then sifted through the beggars cuddling their
infants as they lay in the street, cradling their bodies with
obscene tenderness: I saw them as if for the first time in all
their particularity. Even the laundry, open to the street and
with a gold sign, *Suripong*, appeared something *other than a
laundry.*

•

They say Bangkok is not a city but a collection of ten thousand villages. But each one is as dense, as impossible to decipher as your average city. I walked up to Thong Lor every
day and read all its signs: for Thonglor Massage, with two
images of feet with eyes painted on the toes; for the Suttirjn

furniture store, where a whole gold-laquered pavilion like a tomb stood in the window. Not far away were the wedding parlors for which Thong Lor is famous, in particular the Wedding Castle, which posts an amorous gold statue outside, and a place called the Marriage Studio on Soi 9, fancied up with mannequins in hideous white tuxedos. I began to like it, this Avenue of Matrimony. The wedding parlor consists of a lavish reception area where the young couple are sat down under a chandelier and presented with a wedding catalogue which they can use to plan the whole thing out. Other establishments have names like The Lovers, In Love, and Classic, and in them you can watch the rising middle class planning their weddings by night. They stand there with their gelled hair, surrounded by heart-shaped red balloons, and you wonder what considerations of the future are running through their minds as they fill out their marriage questionnaires. They are Buddhists investing themselves in the symbolism of Christian unions.

•

Thong Lor is so long that it quickly seems a village unto itself, and as part of my recuperation from epiglottitis I forced myself to walk a little farther along it every day. Eventually, I was recognizing as familiar a pharmacy called Fascino which had a whole range of collapsible wheelchairs in its front window, secretive malls and construction sites cloaked in cement powder, cranes and rotting canals, and the Baskin-Robbins outlet done up in *Barbarella* pink. Soon I came to be distracted by the same things. By an apartment tower called the Panjit, for example, which broadcasted— halfway up its side—the simple word NOAH on one of its windows. It always stopped me in my tracks, this word NOAH, and as I stood between all the wedding parlors coughing in the cement dust, I stared at that word NOAH and wondered what it was doing there. Similarly, I was always taken by a bar somewhere near Soi 10 which was devoted to jilted lovers, and inside which patrons could pin up photographs of their faithless ones and hurl glasses at them while songs of despair were played.

I soon found the open-plan mall where Kitty did her grocery shopping, and I used it for the Iberry ice cream parlor on the ground floor where an invalid could rest up with a garcenia or a guava-salted plum sorbet. It was now past Christmas but hymns still hummed in the air. In the parking lot, a Father Christmas still lumbered around in ninety-degree heat, the nylon beard on his unemployed *farang* face coming away like a skin disease. The palms withered around a Crabtree & Evelyn outlet. I would sometimes wait here exhausted, unable to move myself, until night fell. Then, with the heat falling, I could move again.

I have since understood that Thong Lor is the most mysterious of Bangkok streets. Even its green traffic signs, which you see all over the city written in English, are here more cryptic. One reads "Tumble Tots," and a few feet away another reads "Embassy of Khazakstan, 100 meters." The signs are formed like arrows pointing up tiny side streets. In the 55th Plaza, I sometimes ate alone in an always-empty restaurant called Zen. I am an easy believer in the latent meanings of urban signs.

And when night came, the yellow stick neons in the dead trees came on, and the sellers of fake watches came out along with the mobile *maeng-da* buffets (I no longer partook), and the key-makers and dry cleaners and pharmacies with tanks of lemonade-colored water came alive. Even the blue plastic telephone booths of the TRUE company, with that English word emblazoned on their sides, could not be more playful.

•

I believe that Thong Lor was part of my cure. The closer it approaches the Saen Saeb canal the more eccentric it becomes. At the halfway point stands the Thong Lor police station, where, at night, the paddy wagons and a few hookers stand peacefully under large trees which seem to have survived from an earlier age. Here you can easily recall that in 1960 two canals ran side by side the length of the avenue. Designer malls like Playground have also sprung up here, offering new civic spaces for the upwardly mobile classes and their young. Playground is a sharp, rectangular object made of black stone, inside which the stores are arranged around an open space. In front of it students always seem to be erecting goofy artworks out of colored Play-Doh. I found a wooden mosque as large as a doll's house; a complex of Munchkin houses with a restaurant scaled to the height of imaginary midgets. Tudor beams, neoclassic ruins, gold garudas, minarets, Bauhaus lines, marble banks. I like not knowing what these things are or what they mean. I like struggling along streets which are broken and torn, which are hostile to pedestrian instincts.

•

A month went by visiting Thong Lor and soon I was calling it my street. I went later and later at night and ate *yakiniku* in the open-grill Japanese places near the junction, or *guay-tio naam* soup with *sen lek* noodles at the Soi 38 street market around the corner, with a cold *naam sapporot paan*—pineapple juice with crushed ice—sucked through a clogged straw. I still had to wear shades at night, because for some reason—perhaps a sensitivity induced by the medications—I couldn't endure the night lights of Thong Lor or the sting of construction dust in the air. It was January, the best time in Bangkok, clear and bearable at sundown, and the city was wracked with demonstrations against Prime Minister Thaksin, "the Thai Berlusconi" as the scornful middle classes loved to dub him.

Sometimes as I sat near the entrance to Soi 38 with my noodle soup doused with sugar and vinegar, sweating in a gentle and constant way, I would see columns of protesters making their way down Sukhumvit Road in tall orange Dr. Seuss hats, with English placards that read "Thaksin = Evil of Thailand," and "Theft Doesn't Pay." It struck me that these slogans were designed for a foreign press corps and an outside world that couldn't care less about Thailand's remarkable convulsions that year, and which later on ignored the military coup that eventually resulted. Moreover, to proclaim to Thai politicians that theft didn't pay, when theft was their natural modus operandi and always had been, seemed bravely doomed. It was an explosion of public decency that was unlike any demonstration I had ever seen: drums, face paint, and flags concentrated in crowds of tens of thousands who perpetrated no violence.

The protests went up and down the world's longest road, and I sat there, learning the art of assembling *guaytio naam* with limes, chilies, and cheap sugar—Thailand's national dish, which you'll never find in a Thai restaurant. I liked to sit there alone because I could watch the foreign models on their way to Face Bar, and enjoy the nightly demonstrations without being noticed by either group.

One night I watched the demonstration from the Thong Lor Skytrain, then walked hesitantly down the avenue itself with a pineapple cut in half with a penknife. There was an atmosphere of dangerous electricity, such as D. H. Lawrence once described during a visit to Germany in the twenties, as if the whole city had been plunged underwater for a few hours and subjected to a prolonged electric shock. The faces passing me looked intensified, the eyes maddened and bright, and I supposed that on a million TV sets the demonstrations were being discussed as something unprecedented in so apolitical a country. In a cosmology dominated by Vishnu and a divine king, politics doesn't come easily. And when it does come, the shock is immense. I therefore proceeded carefully, picking my way through excitable throngs, until on a darker stretch of Thong Lor I recognized a white man lumbering along by himself, a can of beer in one hand and a walking stick like my own in the other.

•

Farlo's head was unique, and it could be seen from hundreds of yards away, a hard-boiled head with no frills, no beauty, and no nonsense, a head like an artillery shell, a comparison toward which its owner had no doubt impelled it. It bobbed and weaved, as some heads do. It shone with its military baldness, because the old mercenary could not bring himself to break with austere tradition when it came to hair. Buzz-cut baldness was the style of his youth and he kept to it.

When I crossed paths with acquaintances in Bangkok I was always surprised at how unsurprised they seemed, how unconcerned when presented with the coincidence of running into each other in an arbitrary place. Fancy meeting you here on Thong Lor! Not a bit of it. Farlo shrugged and shook my hand as if we had parted from each other the night before after a card game. It was as if we were all trapped together in the same compound for life and therefore there was nothing surprising at all about colliding on Thong Lor. It was in the order of things.

"Where you going, lad?"

"Just wandering."

"Ay, wandering, eh? Just out for a wee wander, eh?"

He cackled and nudged me as he was wont to do. The nudge said, "I know what ye're after!"

"No, really," I said. "I am wandering up Thong Lor. I have a house nearby. I've been sick. In hospital. I'm making myself better."

His eyes blazed up. "In hos-pital?"

"I had a brush with epiglottitis."

"Ay? Epicenter? Stomach cancer?"

I had no idea what he was talking about. But now I took in more deliberately the insane vibrancy of the eye and the shaking of the right hand. So he was back on the bottle.

"Throat problems," I said.

"Ay, ay, throats. Can't stand them meself."

He looked wildly around the street. Nearby there was a large white gate with the word *Exotica* scrawled across it in imposing letters. Guttering orange fires marked out the soup stalls where the workers huddled with powdered hands.

He lifted a finger toward that curved word.

"I was on my way—it's one of me favorite bars."

In all my dozens of excursions through Thong Lor I had never noticed it.

"Exotica?"

"Ay, the Exotica *club*."

Perhaps it had been built overnight the week before, a fairy castle shaped like a Byzantine church. We walked through the scrolled iron gates and down a long driveway with a high wall. Inside niches, baroque putti played their fiddles on one leg. Eggshell domes rose into the night, supported by Corinthian columns. Was Farlo sure it was not a colonial library? And was it really one of his favorite bars?

"Ay, come here every week. Especially Wednesday night."

He turned and placed a hand on my arm for a moment, but then failed to say anything. He looked quite happy, however. His wife had just given birth to yet another baby up in Samlot.

Exotica beckoned. These places often have an air of Grand Guignol, a style that inscrutable Japanese gentlemen appear to prefer. There was a large, expansive plate-glass door upon which were stenciled two images of Johnnie Walker—who else? Next to it stood a gold-plated menu, like that of a high-end restaurant. Doormen in peaked hats came forward to comfort and reassure us, gloved hands raised to orchestrate our measly and timid desires. Have no fear, they seemed to cry, you are in capable hands here!

We flicked through the menu. It announced "Thai Super-model Special!" Prices were marked to the right.

"A wonder," said Farlo. "It's like buying crab at the market."

"Wednesday-night special," the gloved ones were saying, whisking us inside. "Half-price till nine."

We were not dressed up, but in Bangkok it rarely matters. Behind tinted windows, Exotica offered a large room with a horseshoe bar and a raised orchestra platform, upon which was assembled a Thai jazz band of incredible antiquity, old men in ribbon ties greased to the gills, stroking their basses and trumpets. There was a Japanese party at the far side of the bar, and behind them a frolicksome staircase rose to a velvet landing, along whose wall was ranged a series of Edwardian-style lithographs depicting the female silhouette in varying positions of suggestive repose. Bodies like luxury motorcars, like Alfa Romeos which have just been waxed by subordinates. Inside the lounge, the women were in pale-blue slit-leg togas, as is usually the case, but Farlo seemed averse to their approaches. He didn't necessarily come here for the togas, and they were expensive for a man who entertained no more than two tourists a year at his eco-retreat. No, he was here for a different kick, which might merely have been the horseshoe bar and the geriatric jazz band. Or the sight of the staircase opposite us, up which clients with cocktail glasses climbed in slow motion.

I asked him how the business in Cambodia was going and how his own middle age was progressing.

"Oh, fine, fine. I am liking middle age. No one looks to me for anything. I go tae poker games with the lads; I lose and they congratulate me for it. I have a toorist this year, picked him up at the bar in the Sheraton. An American. He said he wanted to go deer hunting with the Khmer Rouge, so I obliged him."

"I am surprised to see you in Bangkok. I thought you only came here once in a while."

"Are you kidding? I have to prospect for clients. It's only three hours from the border, and she has all the rich arseholes I need. I am hunting for Singaporeans these days. I am trying to lure them with tales of rampant tigers."

"Do you have rampant tigers up there?"

He shook a sad head. "Never seen one. I think the land mines have blown them all up."

"Ah, the land mines."

I knew there was a reason no one went to Farlo's lodge.

"I heard someone say, I think it was McGinnis, that the area around Samlot is the most heavily mined area on planet Earth."

"Ay, but it's dead pretty."

"Farlo, have you ever considered moving your lodge somewhere else?"

"That McGinnis is a lying *bas*stard. It's nae the *most* heavily mined area on planet Earth. That would be the DMZ in Korea."

He snarled as he downed a dainty Mai Tai. The bargain Wednesday-night supermodels had appeared and were closing in on us. It was a spectacle seen in a hundred Bangkok bars at a certain time of the night: a small crowd of gorgeous, improbably robed supermodels converging with vampiric desperation upon a couple of dingy, badly dressed *farang* patrons in stained shirts and sandals who are more interested in their argument and in their drinks than they are in the relentless pincer movements of Beauty. The ugly foreigners are spoiled by a superfluity of beauty, made obtuse by this gratuitous superabundance.

"Yes," I said, "but it must deter ordinary holiday-makers."

"Listen, I dinnae give a shit about ordinary holidaymakers. I'm looking for special souls. Those who'll appreciate

my vision. My place is difficult. That's the charm. I could've
made it in the Sooth of France for fuck's sake, but I dinnae.
I made it somewhere nice and fucked up. That's the whole
point. I put it there *because* of the land mines, nae in spite of
them. You should hear them go off in the morning. It's a
grand sound. Like champagne corks."

And he popped a finger out of his cheek.

"I expect they just sound like land mines, Mickey."

"Nay, they sound like champagne corks."

We drank away. The place filled up and soon it was a
scene. Some of the little Japanese salarymen began dancing
with the discounted supermodels, who spoke their language.
A disco ball started turning above us, and our faces were
picked up by moving spotlights. Farlo seemed to deflate a little. Did he really come here on a regular basis? No one recognized him. But then only money and youth get recognized.
At a certain point, complete anonymity overtakes us, and
people—not just women—look right through us as if we
don't exist.

We respond with instinctive bitterness to this loss of visibility, but we also recognize the first taste of our future
extinction, and we accept it. There will be no reprieve from
now on. But Bangkok is a city which in this instance does,
after all, offer a brief reprieve. It comes via a simple gesture,
which Farlo now executed. The invisible man raises a finger, one could call it the Finger of Assent, which indicates
that after long prevarication and weighing up of the available options, he has decided to become financially available
for the sexual act. This single gesture suddenly makes the
anonymous man highly visible, and within a few seconds he
has returned to the field of play upon which his antics, his

desires, his neuroses, and his dubious tastes are all once again invested with the vitality, the fraudulent importance, of his youth. He finds himself returned to life, and his detestable anonymity evaporates all around him.

Farlo did just this, and before my eyes he came back to life. The pallor fell away from him, he got up and propelled himself by means of a mysterious inner spring toward the staircase, where a woman in a blue tunic waited for him— the two of them were speaking in semaphore, and the digital gesture had been recognized instantly. He had become visible again in the realm of sex, which so cleverly imitates the realm of love. He turned to watch me walking toward the door, and as I paid the bill, which I couldn't really afford, he shot me a wink which confirmed that we were now moving in different dimensions. I pushed myself through the swinging Johnnie Walkers and back down to Thong Lor, subtly bewildered and amused.

That curving, duplicitous street was lit up by signs strung along the tenements, of half-naked women forty feet wide calling our attention to the real estate market. I thought back to the Edwardian lithographs on the wall by the stairs, the women's torsos shaped like cellos, and the green chandelier which had lit up Farlo's bald head as he rose to the heavens with a woman on either side of him. Green? Who would fabricate a green chandelier? And I added to myself, "He's like a rabbit disappearing back into its hat." I walked back up to Sukhumvit and bought a pineapple, then walked home past the Wells School, where a pack of stray dogs attacked me in the dark.

Just southeast of Thong Lor lies the neighborhood of On Nut, a sprawling no-man's-land where the servants and chauffeurs who service the Thong Lor palaces have their lodgings. Early in the morning you see these darker-skinned armies of help disembarking from the windowless buses which roar down Sukhumvit Road all the way from On Nut. They look like a slightly different race and in them I recognized the staff of our house on Soi 51, wide and copper-hued, wearing pro-Thaksin T-shirts that winter to remind the upper middle classes for whom they worked that they, at least, were in favor of the flamboyant crook who showered them with government favors.

As they poured down the leafy *soi* where their employers' mansions stood, they sometimes raised two fingers to me in a V sign. It was a proletarian code for "Thaksin Number Two," for the prime minister was listed in the second position on the national ballot sheets and that flashed sign was a defiant insubordination toward their enlightened masters. The latter would often say, at luxurious parties in luxurious gardens, and speaking in English so that the proles hovering nearby with the trays of canapés and champagne flutes wouldn't understand them, "You know, the ordinary people are so appallingly stupid. Thaksin gives them money and government assistance and they all adore him." And I would think, "You mean, they're dumb for taking the money instead of knowing their place in your *fête champêtre*, where they're paid a dollar a day?" And because they all lived in On Nut, which was convenient for the buses down Sukhumvit, the masters themselves rarely ventured into On Nut unless they had to buy a Christmas tree at the giant Tesco there, or make a foray to the equally giant Carrefour which had opened nearby in recent years. But I of course began to walk there frequently when I was tired of Thong Lor.

It's a long walk to On Nut, but you pass through places like Ekkamai, where the great bus station stands and where a number of secretive streets turn themselves into pleasure gardens at night. Sukhumvit turns quiet and brooding after Thong Lor, more Thai, and its exhausting, repetitively asphalt nature comes to the fore. Small hardware stores alternate with showrooms, bathroom equipment outlets, and pharmacies. At night the sidewalks look black, like flows of lava, and halfway to Ekkamai you pass a massive head with a spiked crown, a Greek titan of some kind who announces the Coliseum Club—he is holding a tankard of beer.

"Tartarin," wrote Joseph Roth in his travel book about France, *The White Cities*, "found Marseilles more perplexing than Africa," and this was why. For elsewhere Roth writes something delicate as he explores "the white cities" of southern France: "I won't live to see the beautiful world in which every individual can represent in himself the totality, but even today I can sense such a future as I sit in the Place de l'Horloge in Avignon and see all the races in the world shine in the features of a policeman, a beggar, a waiter."

I thought of that as I hobbled down Sukhumvit beyond

Ekkamai and entered the edges of On Nut, where the hyper-
markets are alive at dusk, their acres of floor space shining
with waxed grapefruits and mango clones, the avenues
around them bursting with neon. The feeling of anonymity
is intense, but the faces possess the same possibility that
Roth saw in Avignon seventy years ago. All is hurly-burly,
motion, greed for life, exacerbation, cynical wonder, eloquent haste, precipitation toward nothing.

By the On Nut station there was a long wall and revolv-
ing ads for Titus watches that I had seen that month all over
the city: *Fun Without Reasons*. From there I could walk
slowly up to Soi 79 and the Sukhumvit Garden City. The
side streets on the way were cramped and hard, but down
one of them one can find an old school called Saint
Michael's, now a kindergarten for the upper middle classes,
with a geometric glass dome and a colonnaded rotunda with
Corinthian capitals. Dead trees all around, old Thai houses
and spirit houses, a fishing tackle shop at the corner of
77 1/2, the old TOT telecommunications building peeling in
relentless humidity. Saint Michael's, in particular, is one of
Bangkok's more mysterious edifices, for there is such a wide
discrepancy between its architecture and its function. It
looks like a Masonic temple, an observatory, a bombastic
hospital, and its grounds swarm with black butterflies.
Standing at the end of this cul-de-sac, I would wait for the
dome to revolve, to part and reveal a giant gun or antenna.
One thinks: What was this forty years ago, fifty years ago,
sixty? Were there jungles all around? Gigantic takian trees of
forgotten forests?

The largest street in On Nut is Soi 77. You can walk for
miles down Soi 77 without knowing where you are. The

ground floors of the tenements are filled with courtyard markets swarming with plastic and bright things, with basil and
cilantro. I sometimes looked in those crowds for our maids
and groundsmen, because this was where they doubtless
shopped, and near Soi 7 and 77 I thought I saw them making their way to the Wat Mahabute temple which sits there
alongside a dark canal. Half-familiar faces among a multi-
tude, tensed in an act of homage.

The Mahabute, after all, is the most famous place in On
Nut and occupies in the imagination of the Bangkok working class an incomparable place as the site of Thailand's
most famous and gruesome ghost story, that of the female
spirit Mae Nak. On Soi 7, the supernatural suddenly erupts,
taking the accidental pilgrim back to a past which can only
be remembered with the greatest difficulty.

•

If Bangkok has renounced her past, physically destroying it
in the process, it is the supernatural which holds her to it
again. There are shrines in the city which are so intense, so
passionate, that they bend time backward and bend us with
it. They are irresistible for this reason, and they remind us
that faith is not merely an entering into superstition, into a
landscape of fear, but a longing for the dead, for the past.

The Mae Nak shrine is draped with *khanom* garlands,
submerged in incense smoke. Into the canal that runs beside
it pilgrims liberate the eels and fish which they buy as
karma-improving offerings from vendors nearby. It is lovely
to watch them kneel by the water's edge and pop open the
plastic bags containing the animals, then watch them swim
away—the latter startled, probably, and confused by their

sudden good fortune. For a few baht you are given a devotional package to dispose of while you are in the temple: a card with a stamp-sized gold leaf, an incense stick, orchids, yellow candles, and mangos. The shrine itself is piled high with toys, diapers, candies, shampoo bottles, model fire engines, teddy bears, lipstick, and at its center is a gold figure of Mae Nak, its skinlike surface softened by constant applications of oil. Devotees kneel before this figure, then gingerly approach to apply small patches of gold leaf to it. A television set, turned on around the clock, faces her, bathing the gold leaf face with electronic light, though it is not clear why Mae Nang needs to watch TV.

More than twenty films have been made of Mae Nak's story, as well as a major opera by the Thai composer Surwong. Believers claim that she is buried in the wat, though they are not sure where. And though Mae Nak is supposed to have been a real person, no one knows quite which part of the mid-nineteenth century can claim her. Some say that she lived during the reign of Rama IV (1851–1868), others that she died during that of Rama V (1868–1910). Mae Nak, the daughter of a village chief in this suburb of Bangkok (it would have been farmland around 1850) falls in love with a commoner named Nai Maak, whom her father despises. Overcoming all obstacles, she manages to marry. Nai Maak, however, is then conscripted into the army and is forced to leave. While he is away, the teenage girl dies during childbirth, and her unborn baby perishes with her. When Nai Maak returns from his military service, the ghost of Mae Nak is there to greet him, weaving a supernatural illusion around their destroyed family life. The illusion is shattered only when one day Nai Maak sees his wife reach for a fallen mango on the earth beneath their house by passing her hands through the floorboards.

It's a theme common to Asian folktales: the dead wife who greets her returning husband as if she were alive, reminding Westerners of the ghost sequences in Mizoguchi's *Ugetsu*, or the first tale in Kobayashi's *Kwaidan*, in which an impoverished samurai's wife, abandoned by her social-climbing husband for a great lady, haunts the house they once shared. Mae Nak also haunts her husband, pursuing him with a mix of desperate love and vengeful jealousy until her spirit and that of her dead child are finally laid to rest by a Buddhist holy man. Nai Maak had taken refuge in the Mahabute temple in what is now On Nut, and the harrying ghost had followed him there. In some versions it is the venerated Somdej Phra Puttajan of Thonburi who seizes Mae Nak's tormented spirit, seals it in a ceramic pot, and throws it into a river.

But Mae Nak sightings do not stop there; she is seen all over Bangkok by the faithful, and it is widely believed by those who play the lotteries that she is an infallible guide to success. The temple is full of fortune-tellers and lottery hopefuls who crowd around the two sacred wax-spotted takian trees there, searching for mystic signs that will point to combinations of numbers. Come here on the day before the national lottery is drawn and you will be unable to get in. The takians (*Hopea odorata*) are mobbed, their surfaces smoothed by dried latex which has oozed out of a hundred cracks in the bark, and it is by rubbing this arboreal surface that lottery aspirants hope to be informed of winning numbers by Lady Takian, the female spirit who inhabits takian trees.

It shouldn't be surprising that tree spirits are worshiped alongside the spirit of a tormented village girl of the nineteenth century. There are Chinese gods here, too, and a glass coffin bearing a figurative "golden child," or *kuman thong*, a spirit who is thought to be a reincarnation of fetuses aborted in previous lifetimes. These charms used to be made of actual dead infants preserved in glass bottles (other, man-made, figures of the *kuman* are shown sucking their own placenta). The *kuman thong* spirit can possess little girls and make them speak for it, and the charm itself can be carried around like a real infant; it whispers into your ear. In the papers you will find occasional stories of mentally disturbed people being arrested for stealing or procuring fetuses in hospitals in order to turn them into *kuman thong*. The dutiful are supposed to appease this spirit and send it back to its rightful mother, the river goddess. They do this by means of a ceremony called "bury with love." The effigy is buried with flowers, and told lovingly that there is no more use for him on earth. There is a charming variation known as "float with love," where it is sent off down a river like a boat. Animism swirls through the city's undergrowth, feeding it from below.

•

What is this mood that takes us as we cut through streets subtly infected with the spirit of Lady Takian? For one thing, the genders seem less divided here than elsewhere in the world. More artfully blended into each other, as if everyone is subconsciously aware that you can be reborn, reincarnated as either gender. Indeed, the very word "gender" seems like a mistake.

I feel Si Ouey snapping at my heels, and I feel the forests of the last century hiding just behind the ubiquitous *Dipterocarpus* trees. These are forces felt only deep inside the body. It is like the force field of a woman who passes you in the dark, like magnetic disturbances that alter a few molecules deep inside your liver.

My walks through On Nut late at night are like séances. In the house on Soi 51, I will hear the banana trees flapping slowly against the double glazing as the servants' table is being set up under the oil lamp slung from a pole where they eat *gai massamam* every night with tin bowls of *kao suay*. A terrible sadness comes over me as I hear those leaves and glimpse the twinkling spirit house through the trees, the crumbling marigolds laid there, and the incense sticks trailing wisps of smoke. The mood suddenly changes. As the spirits move, a supernatural breeze stirs a chime, a bough, or a piece of grit against my tongue—and there for a second I feel them, shrilling like pipes in the distance, flickering in the dark with the mosquitoes.

Thais are never surprised when I admit these feelings to them, since they themselves accept them as perfectly normal. For them it would be abnormal *not* to feel the closeness of the dead, to search for another past vastly different from the physical one.

Weeks went by, and finally the rains came. I lay in my glass house, trying to learn the Thai script, watched by the staff as they pruned the frangipani trees. Learning the curves of that variant of Sanskrit, but never really learning it properly, was a healing exercise in a sort of futility, for deep down I suspect I wanted to remain in day-to-day incomprehension relative to the language, which I never learned to speak well. It was like a soft wall enclosing me at all times, and I preferred for many reasons not to penetrate it too adroitly. There was something Chaplinesque in the episodes of mutual incomprehension that delighted me no end.

When a severe humidity arrived with the first rains and the glass house heated up, I found myself wanting to take cold baths. Unfortunately, the plug in my bath was broken and I couldn't fill the tub. I called Kitty. What is Thai for "plug"? She had no idea. Dictionaries, calls to friends, forays to libraries yielded no help. No one knew. I went to the Kinokuniya bookstore in the Emporium Mall, a few blocks away and spent a morning searching high and low for the Thai word for "plug." No result. Finally I took the plug itself and wandered down to a hardware store on Sukhumvit Road. I dangled the magic object in front of my face and asked them what it was in Thai. The entire staff came out and looked at me as if I were mad. The owner pointed at it and said, "*Pluk.*" I repeated it after him. *Pluk.* They all shook their heads. Not *"pluk."* *Pluk.* Or was that *Plukghk?* Or *Prukk?* *"Pluk,"* I said. They all shook their heads again. No, no, not like that. *Pluk.* Couldn't I hear it? Listen. *Plukkk.*

I bought a dozens pluks and stored them from then on in the bathroom. But every other day I'd wander down to different stores and ask for a pluk. For two weeks no one understood the word. Then, one fine day, I asked for a pluk in the Villa Supermarket and the sales guy went and got it for me without a murmur. So my mouth and my ear had finally aligned. That is how long it takes to master Thai. It was the same for the words for noodle soup, *guaytio naam.* Since it can be eaten only on the street, there is no menu you can point to. You have to ask for it orally. On Soi 38, I asked for it every day for the better part of a fortnight before tongue and ear finally lined up the tones properly. Four weeks, two words: "plug" and "soup."

Vital words, but how about "disoriented," or "alone"? Armed with a bare dozen words, I could forage, feed, and bathe myself. But I couldn't enter into the treacherous subtleties of human relations, and perhaps I didn't want to. No one ever truly appreciates how much Robinson Crusoe enjoyed his solitude. My glass house and gardens were an island of sorts—they *looked* like a tropical island—and the principal difference between Crusoe and a Bangkok transplant in the early twenty-first century was the staff hanging about with their pruning shears, peering in through the glass walls at Farang Exhibit A as he dabbled with calligraphy on a sofa bed. The children in particular were grimly fascinated. They hung in the trees, eating peaches and staring.

•

When suffocated, I simply walked down Sukhumvit to the Emporium Mall near Phrom Phom. As of then, it was the newest and most formidable of the city's malls, a snapshot of an Asian future dominated by the color white. I took the zigzag escalators up, through a central space filled with a soaring abstract Christmas tree made of multicolored metal leaves. For me, no tablecloths from Versace on the ground floor, or items from the Beverly Hills Polo Club and Sport Chic. On the fourth floor, however, was a toy store called Be Cute which I liked to browse through, and from which I often bought strange Japanese sweets which I never ate but which sat on my sideboard for weeks before being thrown out. I liked them, I suppose, purely for their names. Hello Kitty and Hi-Chow, then Cola tablet candies and jackfruit chips. The nauseating cuteness of Japanese capitalism. More fascinating, and nauseating, still was Born in Japan, filled with plastic toys called Flip Flops—a plant with two leaves that bobbed up and down to music. There were times when the whole display bobbed to bossa nova and the children there did the same, all bobbing in synchronicity with these mechanical toy plants. And so, sated with Japan, I would wander on, through curved thoroughfares of plate glass, through isles of artificial rain forest, through amenities worthy of a Biosphere or those hub airports with which Asia now leads the consumer world. Announcements in silky Japanese rose above the din. The brands are so spatially condensed that they soon form a verbal ribbon inside one's head. You begin to fiddle with your wallet. Anonimo, Blancpain, Bossini (the brightest store on earth), Adidas, Georges

Rech, Rampage. Apex Profound Beauty. Kitahachi Udon. Baume & Mercier. It is a new language, the patois of brands. The Germans naturally have a brilliant word for it: *Konsumterrorismus*.

There was one place inside Emporium where I could make my solitude. It was the corner where the Royal Davinci furniture showroom met the Ellezza Crystal and Symphony store. The windows of these two shops gave out onto a darker-than-usual stretch of corridor where there were benches for tired itinerants. The showrooms were dense, packed with the whole gamut of bad European taste from the incomparably vulgar 1860–1914 period. The period of effulgence, boasting, raw confidence, and venal exotica. I could only marvel at the Third Empire mirrors stacked here waiting for some Thai millionaire to drag them back to his *satai roman* mansion. Or the gold elephant clocks, the gilt hat stands, the naval paintings, and the cut-glass gondoliers with crystal boatmen in top hats. There was even a 3-D rendering of Klimt's *Kiss*, which shimmered as if about to explode. It went quite well, one would have to concede, with the glass elevators nearby and the Arab pop music. But most eye-catching of all was a display placed right in the middle of this fourth-floor street. It consisted of a glass pavilion framed by tasseled sashes and lit from inside by a chandelier. Within was a single case of antique "1805" Johnnie Walker, the "Jewel of Whisky." It was surrounded by a Victorian writing case with period nib pens and a leather recipe book supposedly once belonging to Alexander Walker, Johnnie's grandson. On the cover of this curious book, plain to see, were three words which I imagine were the reason for my stopping here every time I came to the mall, and which were even more striking than the bearskin adorning the shrine's floor, namely: "Where is it?"

•

When I came back down, I walked alone to the Phrom Phom Skytrain station, climbing up to the station gallery, where a few outlets were still selling fresh beetroot juice and cassettes of Green Music. Unlike Asoke or Nana, this station is near empty at night. I walked up the left side of Sukhumvit, where I knew all the places: the golf equipment outlet with its Cobra clubs and Power Tornado drivers, the furniture store with the longest store name you have ever encountered (Pipithsampavararit), filled with gilded, looted *apsaras*. The Sukhumvit Toyota dealership, with its awkward English slogans probably translated literally from Japanese: *Are You Groovy? Yes! My Life Party.* And, next to an Innova model: *Big Memories.*

By a tailor called Bitharo, there was a string of barbershops with names like Lek Barber and On Salon, rooms set back from the street with murals of idyllic villages in Issan and portraits of the king and queen colored like Hindu saints. I went into Lek. Any hair salon with the name "Small" is a provocation to a *yak*. So I sat in the beaten chair of greasy burgundy leather and, for the hell of it, got myself shaved as well. I came out smelling of rancid pomegranates, and, looking across the street, spied the tailor called Beethoven which McGinnis had mentioned all those summers ago. A Beethoven suit? *I say, is that a Beethoven suit?*

The Rex Hotel was lit up like a dismal roadside motel in Oklahoma, bald *farang*s in the coffee shop windows. I would always stop for a while and wonder why I never ventured down the side street Soi 33, although since Livingstone's was situated here it was familiar to me. Late at night, the girls who work there flow down to Sukhumvit in search of cabs, and you see at once the difference between them and the denizens of Nana and Soi Cowboy. They have a different look: I could swear they were a little taller, a bit more sophisticated, a bit better dressed. But I did know that the bars of Soi 33 were themed preponderantly around classic French painters. Surely this fact alone suggested a better class of clientele, unless you assume that every Tom, Dick, and Harry knows who Degas was, though I wouldn't bet on it. Bangkok rumor had it that the Manet club had turned into the Monet club because of a sign painter's error, but either way, one had to admire the effort of bringing such a level of cultural consciousness to Asia's erotic tourists. They would go home enriched. Nevertheless, I stood there hesitating, because if the truth be known I dislike going to a bar by myself, even in the bar capital of the world. But as soon as McGinnis discovered that I lived in the vicinity of one of his favorite streets, invitations to join him there began to flow over the telephone.

•

"I have a friend," he said one night, "who you must meet. He's my only French friend, Lionel. Do you know Lionel? Lionel's a legend."

"I don't know any legends, I'm glad to say. And I'm even happier to report that I don't know any Lionels."

"But Lionel is different." He mispronounced the name, emphasizing the first vowel in the English way. *Li-onel*. "Lionel's one of the funny uncles."

"Oh, the guys who sell you drugs? I don't—"

"Come on, Lalant, don't be such a bore. I'm not suggesting a drugfest. I think we should go to Soi 33 and soak up some culture. With Lionel. Lionel's a wonderful pervert. He's French. He knows Soi 33 back to front, top to bottom. Especially bottom."

We had a weary chuckle. "All right. Where are you now?"

"End of the street, old man. We're having a cappuccino at the Cal Tex."

For a moment my heart sank, but there it was, I had to invite them round. It was the first interruption of my months of solitude.

"Are you alone?" he muttered.

One could never underestimate McGinnis's paranoia. It was one of the most fragrant things about him, but from where did it originate?

"I live in a household," I said. "My landlady is having a cocktail party right now."

"Landlady? Cocktail party?"

He conferred frantically with the mysterious Lionel.

"Are you both stoned?" I asked.

"Not at all, not at all. Lionel and I are *not* stoned. We are merely diplomatic."

"Maybe I should come and get you."

"No, we want to see where you live."

"We?"

"Yes. Lionel is as curious as I am."

"I don't know Lionel."

He hung up. Five minutes later they were at the door. I had not been lying, and there was indeed a cocktail party going on in the main house. Well-dressed Thais and *farang*s of obvious wealth swanned about in the brightly lit windows of the salon. The maid came to my door, looking a little concerned.

"There are two men for you outside, sir. They look like tramps. Shall I let them in?"

My heart sank even further. The disadvantage of my household arrangement was that everyone could see, and inspect, everyone. And I felt an absurd social concern, namely that the staff would think badly of me as I entertained these two aging drug addicts who had wandered down so nonchalantly from the gas station espresso bar. One is sometimes capable of astonishingly shameful acts of cowardice. I went down to meet them under the umbrous mango trees, where hopefully we would all be invisible. Lionel was tiny, barely five feet tall, and he wore an extravagantly wide collar like a twenties intellectual, paired disastrously with khaki shorts. He looked like an evil child, with sandy hair brushed all over to one side as if covering up a wound. He shook my hand limply. McGinnis was in baggy pants, a crinkled shirt which had seen better days, and—horror of horrors—espadrilles. With his mountain of hair, he looked vaguely like an English poet on sabbatical in Majorca circa 1960. He was deeply tanned and his skin glowed like the inside of a peach hastily bitten. From the house came a sound of exaggerated laughter and the tinkle of forks clashing with china. McGinnis took it all in in one second.

"Thai aristocracy," he whispered. "Fascist bastards."

"Her grandfather was a famous general—"

"They're all like that. Ties to the dictatorship!"

Lionel nodded—but which dictatorship?

At that moment the maid thoughtlessly turned on the

lawn lamps and we were suddenly exposed like three men escaping from Colditz. I hustled them in toward the pool, but we were spotted by the giggling socialites. I was grateful McGinnis didn't give them the finger.

"A pool," he cried instead. "May we bathe?"

"Bathe? There's a party going on. They'll be watching."

"I want to bathe among the fascist bastards."

"They're not fascist bastards, McGinnis. They're perfectly nice socialites."

"But that is a contradiction in the terms," the pervert said in appalling English. "They are *aristocrates*."

"So is your little English friend," I hissed at him. "What the fuck is that supposed to mean?"

But he simply grinned and drew a finger across his throat. McGinnis had slipped into the house and undressed down to his underpants, in which he reemerged into the frangipani gardens picked out by a dozen spotlights, a statue illustrating the sadness of mortal flesh. The guests watched him walk to the edge of the pool and then, with that gesture of imminent flight which I had observed in him before, take wing in a grotesque dive contrived expressly for their benefit. A loud crash interrupted the conversation and at the center of the floodlit pool an Englishman in advanced decay appeared like Piss Christ. "Oh my god," someone said from the salon. "He's going to drown."

"Not so," came the booming voice. "Good evening to you. I am Earl McGinnis, B. Phil. Cantab. Cantab being the rarest and most expensive melon known to English greengrocers. You doubt me? I am here to recite a poem for you, it being such a lovely evening and you all in ties. I have some aristocratic poems for you. Poems written by one of our foremost earls."

They came to the windows, and everyone was apparently interested.

" 'A Ramble in Saint James's Park,' " McGinnis began, and his voice was authoritative, musical, and cutting. There are defining moments in every friendship, and even in every acquaintanceship, moments when another's critical faculties are admirably exposed by a sudden flight of the tongue. I immediately understood that Saint James's Park in Rochester's poem was, for the reciter, Bangkok itself. No one understood a word of it except me.

> *Much wine had passed, with grave discourse*
> *Of who fucks who, and who does worse*
> *(Such as you usually do hear*
> *From those that diet at the Bear),*
> *When I, who still take care to see*
> *Drunkenness relieved by lechery,*
> *Went out into St. James's Park*
> *To cool my head and fire my heart.*
> *But though St. James has th' honor on 't,*
> *'Tis consecrate to prick and cunt.*
> *There, by a most incestuous birth,*
> *Strange woods spring from the teeming earth;*
> *For they relate how heretofore,*
> *When ancient Pict began to whore,*
> *Deluded of his assignation*
> *(Jilting, it seems, was then in fashion),*
> *Poor pensive lover, in this place*
> *Would frig upon his mother's face;*
> *Whence rows of mandrakes tall did rise*
> *Whose lewd tops fucked the very skies. . . .*

•

"I know every bar," Lionel said as we walked down Sukhumvit toward Soi 33. "I think of this street as my private violin on which I can play anything I want."

"A violin?"

"Yes, a violin."

"Xylophone, more like," McGinnis drawled. "The cheap metal kind you buy at the supermarket for a hundred baht."

"You misunderstand my metaphor."

McGinnis, one of the great Francophiles, put an orangutan arm around Lionel.

"You wide-headed French twat, there is no metaphor I do not understand. There are, indeed, few I do not thrill to. You are a xylophone."

"Ah," said Lionel, as if he understood.

"You mean, I assume, that you are the virtuoso of Soi 33?"

"*Exacte.*"

Soi 33 is a dense and complex street, otherwise called Soi Daeng Udom, or else Dead Artists Street. At its entrance stand a 7-Eleven and the UBC 2 Building, in which can be found the Londoner Brew pub, while a little farther in one passes a club called Christie's, and two restaurants, named Basilico and Pan Pan. Opposite them rises the Novotel hotel and Coco's Café, where I had once spent a Christmas alone when I was staying at the Livingstone. After the Novotel, the dead artist bars begin: Dalí on the left side of the street, Van Gogh, Renoir, Degas, and Gauguin on the right. Farther up are Goya and Monet/Manet, and around them other establishments themed in other veins—Napoleon, Wall Street, Santana, and one called Demonia, a Thai-style S&M joint. Parrot Green, Lookie Lookie, and Big Shots line the small side street of Soi 33/3, and forgo any mention whatsoever of deceased titans of the canvas, though Lookie Lookie was apparently opened as the Mondrian. Big Shots has a brass plaque outside which reads *Non Members Only*. The You and Me Club is self-explanatory.

What attracts one to nosing about in bars is the sudden change of atmosphere that promises the opening of a new door—a new window into life. It's nonsense, but we need nonsense. We went into the Monet, where a middle-aged Japanese man was doing a hula dance on a table. A girl stood by the door, holding an artist's palette, with a mustache painted on her face. A long brush was held parallel to her mouth. "Bo'jow," she whispered as people came in. The red-lit bar sported a lone Monet, one of the water-lily series, and behind it stood lines of half-empty bottles with Thai and Western names scribbled over them, and on several of these the word *Lionel* could be seen. The system on Soi 33 is that the repeat customer can buy a bottle fixed at the bar, have his name put on it and return with mixers and ice anytime he likes and not pay again until said bottle has been finished. If a bottle of Absolut costs about 2,000 baht, the client gets ten to twelve drinks out of this amount, an incredible bargain, which is sure to make him return night after night—the bar, naturally, does not make most of its profit on vodka cocktails. Lionel suddenly came into his own. His sweat, his diminutive stature, awkward hair, and venal grin all magically fell into place and he blossomed visibly into a barfly occupying his rightful niche in the sweeping ecosystem of

Bangkok nightlife. "Afterward," Lionel said, "I am taking you to Christie's to see the six-foot wooden penis in the garden." It was, it appeared, typical of the kinds of announcements he liked to make in male company. I began to warm to his peculiar brand of repulsiveness. Lionel had been a quite well-known journalist in Paris, but he had been a journalist in a country which mostly despises journalists and pays them less than unionized garbage collectors.

Lionel did documentaries about Islamic "problems," reportages on shelters for battered Maghrebian women, reports from the increasingly battered and sabotaged Mediterranean, a sea—as he put it—that was once gay, pagan, vibrant with innocent sex and beauty, but which was now increasingly a grimy, polluted, overpopulated arena of conflict between two mutually antagonistic civilizations. The world, he said, was full of refugees from the Mediterranean, which was once the most beautiful place on earth. The garden of civilization, the preferred abode of writers and artists. The cradle of enlightened hedonism.

"It was only a short time ago," he said as we plucked down one of his bottles of curaçao and mixed our own drinks (and suddenly he was much more interesting, speaking in his native tongue), "that our parents and grandparents flocked to the Mediterranean as an escape from the ghastliness of the North. They went to take off their clothes, to eat properly, to drink properly, to become human again. It was a recognized ritual. Now we go to Luton or Orly and take a charter flight to Goa, the Seychelles, Bangkok, Phuket. Our innocent pleasure gardens are no longer in Europe or America. The sun kisses us at the equator, among images of Buddha and Shiva. Innocent, you say? Bangkok, innocent? Yes.

It is *far* more innocent than Torremolinos, Mykonos, or Miami. Far more innocent than Atlantic City or Catalina or Las Vegas, or even than Malta. After all, what is the idea behind those places now? We feel choked in them. Whereas, I am sorry, but I simply don't feel that here. Perhaps it's merely that here we have *sanuk* and in those other places we don't. Perhaps the West is just a shithole now and there's nothing we can do."

"Canterbury," McGinnis said quietly. "Canterbury is not a shithole."

"I am sure it is, in fact, a shithole at this point. I cannot imagine Canterbury as crucial to the hedonistic imagination."

"Maybe not hedonistic, but—"

Lionel mixed our drinks himself, calmly and knowledgeably. It is quite something to know about drinks, to know about them the way a botanist knows trees and plants. He made them up smoothly, not missing a beat. He was about fifty, a young fifty, and there was nothing wasted or wrinkled about him. After years working the fringes of the Med doing stories about illegal immigration, he had gone to Indonesia and Malaysia to look at the rise of religious extremism in those tense nations.

"Every culture needs a Garden of Eden. I am afraid with the loss of the Med we have lost ours. I think that place was a way of believing in our own innocence, and then finally we couldn't believe in it anymore. The place itself just became so overwhelmingly developed. I drive down to Antibes now, or Monaco, and I cannot believe my eyes. In two generations we have totally fucked it to death. It looks like New Jersey at best. The coastline of Italy or Spain in summer—we

won't even mention France—looks like an industrial accident. So we look farther and farther afield for what we used
to have. It's a journey into the past."

"I am sure," McGinnis put in, "that the past was even
more of a shithole than the present. Isn't that the Asian attitude?"

"Forgive me, but you don't mean that. You of all people.
You are the biggest romancer of the past."

McGinnis turned to me. "Where would *you* go for a
romantic weekend? Lionel here has given up serious journal-
ism and is now writing about spas. He has passes to all of
them. He's always trying to get me to go with him."

"We'll drive in my car," the Frenchman said cryptically.

We then stepped over to Christie's to experience the
man-sized penis in the back garden, where there was also a
tethered horse. The horse looked at the penis and the penis
looked at us. Animism in action. We moved on to Dalí,
which from the outside looks as if it is made of wet spaghetti, like a Frank Gehry nightclub, its line waving and
undulating, which of course was meant to suggest the fluid-
ity of Dalí's objects. Or it could have been the curaçao, of
course. Inside, there were more Dalinian touches. The ceiling
was covered with the master's motifs, and the hostesses wore
excruciating hats which could well have been designed by
him. Lionel had his own bottles here, too. Did he come to
Soi 33 every night?

"I have discovered," he explained, "that the girls on
Soi 33 are unique. Many of them are attending marketing
courses in city colleges. They are all related to each other, or
have the same boyfriends. They are better educated, as you
can sense. The strangest thing, though, is the popularity of

those marketing courses—why would that be, I have often wondered? Is Soi 33 known among marketing undergraduates as a part-time earner? I have often taken one home only to find myself talking about marketing strategies the whole of the next day. Not that I mind. But I have not fathomed why."

"Perhaps," I said, "they are pursuing their studies?"

How many bars can one visit in a single night? On Soi 33, all of them. At Napoleon the girls at the front door stuffed one arm into their tunics as if they had lost them in battle. We went to Renoir. Around the pool table were Edwardian fixtures and lithos of Alfa Romeo racing cars from the thirties, and somehow I ended up revising my opinion of Renoir the more Black Russians I drank. I ended up thinking he was a genius, the greatest of all geniuses and every bar in Bangkok should be themed around his paintings, especially the ones with fields of poppies and girls in straw hats. I was soon positively in love with Renoir, especially as some of the girls wore painter's smocks, and I thought exactly what Lionel now said out loud: "Look, they're Impressionists too!" Lionel was whispering into my ear as if he wanted to know me better. "What part of New York do you live in? Do you like it?"

At the end of Soi 33, past 33 Center and Demonia, stands a shabu place with the most succulent, tiny scallops on earth. It's where the drunkards go when they need to cool off. It's often filled with clients of the spanking show in Demonia, sometimes with spankers and spanked tagging along for a free meal. Suddenly, then, all the violent color and drama of the street's business falls away and once again we are all humble mammals eating shabu scallops together and peering at each other with a kind of evolutionary curiosity. The girls no longer in flowing togas looked like the slightly gaunt marketing undergraduates which they no doubt were. Most of their patrons that night were Asian, which according to Lionel was typical.

"If I have to listen to one more NGO type droning on about *fat, white, middle-aged perverts* I think it will have to be violence. Besides, is it some sort of crime to be white, fat, and middle-aged in a country where you are 0.5 percent of the population? Or what about middle-aged but not fat, or vice versa? I always point out that *farang*s are less than 5 percent of the customers in Bangkok. Get furious about that 5 percent if you want—it says more about you than them."

McGinnis: "Lionel, it is purely aesthetic, that's all. It's like the feelings between blacks and whites. It's irrational."

The scallops restored our zest.

"I think I'll come with you to Hua Hin," I said cheerfully. "Why not? It's free, isn't it?"

"Still didn't get your check, Lalant? Don't worry, I'm broke, too. Lionel?"

"I have passes for Chiva Som, the best spa in Thailand. I have to write a report for a Swiss magazine."

"I used to go a lot with my wife," McGinnis put in unexpectedly. "She spent all my money there."

I said, "Where *is* your wife?"

He shrugged and twirled a marine beast on his fork. Did he pick up and lose wives in a serial way? Or did he invent them for his friends while spending all his life alone?

"I've never seen you with a wife," Lionel snapped. "Good God."

"I went there every other weekend. Lalant, I am surprised you haven't been to Hua Hin yet. It's practically a suburb of Bangkok."

"A three-hour drive. I have a driver, too." Lionel looked quite happy at the prospect. "I will bring my wife, too."

"Your what?"

"Her name is Fon. We got married last month."

A pang of envy seemed to cross McGinnis's face.

"She's not a marketing undergraduate. She's in sales."

"How nice for you."

•

Across the street from the shabu place stood a curious mall built around a courtyard over which the words PEEP INN stood with an ominous gravity all their own. The ground floor was lined with Japanese-only clubs outside of which red paper lanterns and a single hostess stood. As we passed they bowed and said something in Japanese, though we were clearly the wrong race to be so addressed. In the gloom and quiet of this recess, Lionel asked me about New York with more insistence, and I finally admitted that the only parts of New York I could stand now were the immigrant neighborhoods around Sunset Park and Bay Ridge in Brooklyn, which I could reach on the R train and which were now fifty-fifty Hispanic and Chinese, though the Chinese were clearly getting the upper hand. Walking around the Chinese parts of Seventh Avenue near Fifty-ninth Street always reminded me of On Nut in some way. The streets which had changed hands many times, the Chinese grandmas on the stoops watching you go by with eyes that knew you—and the smell of sad trees in summer. But I could never live there.

"Why not?"

"Because I'm not an immigrant."

"That's exactly what you are."

"Yes, but immigration is a patterned affair. Segregated like nothing else."

"Ah well. We are all immigrants here, too. And we live in a ghetto of sorts."

Lionel gestured toward a pair of frosted-glass doors providing entrance to the aforementioned Peep Inn. The frosting formed the shape of a naked girl which any entrance would break into two halves.

"This," he sighed, "is our ghetto."

We didn't go in. Next door was a plush club with girls in flowing Santa hats. Wasn't it rather late in the year for those? It did indeed look like a cranny in a ghetto, and we the stigmatized ghetto denizens were marked out for an easy kill. The madame stepped out with smooth words, disconcerted, it was clear, by our non-Japaneseness.

"Come inside," she said, "it's Christmas special."

The road to Hua Hin crosses a plain covered with watery paddies and scores of small windmills. The skies are spacious outside of Bangkok, the effect of a flat land, and the flyspeck towns with their Honda dealerships and shuttered banks look unnaturally bright even under low clouds. It's a straight road and always busy: the Bangkok middle class follow their king to take the sea air at Hua Hin, as they have since the twenties. And here I was, too, with Lionel, Fon, and McGinnis in a giant boatlike Camry limo commanded by a driver in the usual Thai getup of peaked white hat and gloves. He had been provided by the magazine, which regarded Lionel as a star of some kind, and during the three-hour ride he said nothing to us at all. Was he disgusted by the presence of a beautiful young Thai girl in the midst of this *farang* expedition? I couldn't say. Fon herself was a thirty-year-old operator, as far as I could see, but it was also clear that she and Lionel had come to some sort of troubled arrangement among themselves. Not money for companionship so much as companionship in exchange for promises of a new life, eventually, *elsewhere*. She spoke English and French well, and from time to time she said acidly to the driver, "You took the wrong road. Is he paying you by the hour?" She clearly regarded McGinnis and me with deep suspicion, and I thought that, all in all, that was fair enough.

The weekend stampede to Hua Hin—a cavalcade of

limos and Mercedes shuttered with sunscreens, their back-seats loaded with snoozing fat faces and flapping fans. At times the traffic slows and an atmosphere of impending disaster brews all around. The names of the villages are obscure. The warehouses of textile and software companies shine with their sickly cheap look at the edges of dusty lots, hastily screened by pathetic little trees that don't grow. Bill-boards announce a *Mystery of Siam* that has shriveled up here under the force of prosperity.

We shot past a fairground beginning to light up in the first glows of twilight, the elephants lined up along a rice field with silver masks on their heads, their toenails painted blue. The clouds dripped into slopes of dreary forest, signaling the end of the plains and the first rolling hills. I left the window open and slumped back on the caramel leather, as if trying to suck in air that wasn't refrigerated. It was now a fast, bumpy ride. Water buffalo stood in the dusk, their hides a color of rose ash, enduring the rain. The gutters overflowed, the shops were closed down. People scattered through dusky lanes in waterproof hats. At Hua Hin, the sea was violent, a vast change from the tepid bathwater it usually was. Seaside towns always strike me as the epitome of failure—but at what do they fail?

•

Chiva Som is set on the ocean two miles out of Hua Hin's raffish center. It was an exclusive resort for wealthy health neurotics who can fork out the $500 a night for chalets designed to suggest a Buddhist monastery set around private gardens of flame-vines. It's a world apart, proof of the anxious theorem that money can buy you a suspension of the world's intrinsic tedium and fatigue, and indeed it presents you with the calm geometry of all planned, gated communities, which are utopian by default. It was to this enclosed paradise that Lionel had passes, and like refugees from urban poverty we all suddenly felt relieved, if not overjoyed.

At the lobby, with its curved gables and teak pillars, a "personal guide" was waiting with a tray of orange tea and our keys. The mood was a kind of forced placidity which felt as if it could break into pieces at any moment. Most of the other guests had fled back to Bangkok because of the storm and as a result we would have an exceptional degree of solitude. A manageress came out to *wai* and wish us an agreeable stay. Only the Thai kickboxing classes had been canceled, she said, assuring us that water therapies were still functioning and that the beach was not yet closed.

The resort is so spread out that it has to be navigated in a golf cart with a canopy and rain flaps. We were driven straight to our chalet set in a glade of bamboo, from where the turmoil of the ocean was less palpable. But the bamboo itself shook frenetically. Blown about like Charlie Chaplin, Lionel became imperious and demanded in a shrill voice to be introduced to the managers and the staff, but it was clear that they had never heard of either him or his Swiss magazine, which was called *Loisirs et Mers*, or something like that (or was it *Loisirs de Merde?*) They looked at him with a gentle bemusement, a look of which Thais are masters, and Lionel reacted to this dismissal with a touching pomposity, the pomposity of the man who has come down in the world and who cannot do anything about it.

"He is inspecting me!" he now said to the Thais with ineffectual urgency in his dodgy English.

"Mr. who?"

"I don't know. He's Swiss."

"The manager is in Bangkok, sir. But you have your passes."

"But—" Lionel exploded, "but—"

"All water treatments are free," they replied, closing the discussion. "This way, please."

"Do you realize who I am—the Swiss tourist market—thousands of readers. Well, hundreds anyway—"

It rained hard on the gabled roofs, and in my room I gorged on the small chocolates and snacks presented at bedside in a miniature basket. From time to time a low *boom* wafted across the toy-town paths and gardens from the sea, and it was not a comforting sound. The fan cooled the bed on which I lay, and yet somehow I could not relax. I was Hansel with no Gretel, trapped in the magic cottage. I had come, in truth, just to get a free buffet. Foolish, I knew. A weekend with two madmen. In the future I would choose both my friends and my weekends more wisely.

•

A little later, I went for a swim in the spa pool, which was placed a few feet from the beach behind a long wall staked with flowering trees. The latter had now all been stripped of petals, and they vibrated in their grim nudity as the sea winds mocked them. The pool was ordinarily strewn with rose petals, but these had now been blown into a heap in one corner; the tables had been blown over, the chairs tossed to and fro. A waiter struggled to weight down a tablecloth with four ashtrays. As napkins flew through the air he leaped up to catch them, as if these balletic movements were part of his sad duties. As the rain finally eased, and a greasy light shot through the heavens, I paddled about in the petals. It was ironic that, while I often thought of myself as trying to escape the West and its follies, I usually ended up in a swimming pool reserved almost exclusively for my own race. Soon, however, it was dinnertime.

The restaurant was on the second floor, an Ayurvedic buffet with cumin-sprinkled boiled eggs thrown in to appease the frustrated carnivores. The idea behind the spa was to control one's intake of calories to a bare minimum determined on the day of one's arrival by the in-house nutritionist. Fortunately, the guy had fled to Bangkok and the buffet therefore seemed morally aimless. The waiters lit a candle for us; the windows rattled and whined. Lionel and McGinnis, against all odds, had dressed in jackets and ties, paradoxically appropriate in this spare, high-minded decor, and we broke open a bottle of Evian while speaking in whispers, as one often does in a totally empty space.

"Evian?" McGinnis gasped.

"Well, it will improve your liver, at least. It's a spa. It's supposed to be healthy."

"Holy Buddha. Evian. Do you see, Miss Lalant? And you have to *pay* for it."

"Drinks are not included."

"There are no drinks. Evian is not a drink, sir. Can we get a health martini?"

As we sat there, pieces of detritus sailed past the windows, and one of these was a garden chair. The chef came out and laughed, but not with any jollity. The sea was playing up; a few waves had hit the wall. Lionel flinched and his eyes darted up at me. There was something tense and difficult between us that had not yet been defused, and for a moment his eyes were not blue at all but a savage violet, like poisonous flowers whose color warns off birds. He stared straight into me and I could not for the life of me recognize who was looking at me. He called over to the idling staff. "Martinis?"

They shook their heads in the gloom.

Mercifully, management had come to some kind of conclusion and music started up on the sound system. It was the Green Music from the Skytrain, all flutes and gamelans and yogurt pots, the music of inner peace and growing grass and liquid spirulina. The sound, I always thought, of cows strenuously thinking. Now it made us feel like cows thinking, which I suppose was the idea. Lionel gripped his fork until his knuckles went white, and he was so perfectly still that I began to feel an accumulating, serious alarm. And what was it all about? I kept thinking as quickly and nimbly as I could. This rage, rising closer and closer to the surface, like blood from an underwater duel, a cloud of redness and sorrow and filth. In response to these events, McGinnis, keeping his cool, took out his mechanical tree frog, placed it on the table, and activated the spring, whereupon it began to chatter away. Lionel gave a start.

"What is that?"

"It's my mademoiselle magnet. Sooner or later, a beautiful woman always appears and asks me what it is."

"What is it, then?"

"I'll tell you later. You're not a beautiful woman."

"No," Lionel snapped, "but if you remember, I am a reliable source of them."

"And where is Fon?" I asked.

"Asleep. She sleeps all the time."

There was such wretchedness in Lionel's statement that we fell silent. Men can come to a standstill in this way before your very eyes. Fascinating. Are we all the same in this regard? Was it because (I was feeling a tad pessimistic that evening) all our cherished relationships fail to pan out as we anticipate? But it could also have been because the scene around us was so unusually dispiriting. I imagine that Chiva Som is usually an optimistic sort of place, because it is surely optimistic to get people to eat alfalfa for a week and make them lose weight. The kickboxing classes, the thalassotherapy, the Greco-Roman water suites, the nutritionists— and people flew all the way to Bangkok for this. The empty resort looked so obviously like an outpost of Western values imposed upon a native background. At the gates, guards. Around the walls, more guards. From whom, then, were we being protected? For Lionel the answer was obvious: the Muslims.

I confess that the exaggerations which inevitably flow when this line of thought is opened up always fatigue me. But it was difficult to deny that something peculiar was happening in this part of Southeast Asia. The government was reeling, the military was waiting in the wings to take over— as it eventually did—and the war in the south was precipitating everything, transforming the state from within. And the Bangkok authorities were losing control of this dirty war against an Islamic insurgency in their southernmost provinces on the Malaysian border. Buddhist monks were being beheaded; drive-by shootings, even of Muslims by their own radicals, were so common they were no longer news. Bombings, ambushes, soldiers killed, thousands of casualties: no society can remain unchanged by such things happening inside it. Perhaps the Thailand we knew was on borrowed time.

"Everything has changed this year," Lionel said, lowering his mouth so that the staff wouldn't hear, though who knows if they might not have agreed with all of it. He grew icily animated. "Buddhists and Muslims have lived together for generations, but now we are seeing an ethnic cleansing of Buddhists in the South. The villages are separating, the two communities are coming unstuck, dividing into wounded, mistrustful camps, Muslims in one village, Buddhists in another. The symbiosis has come apart. It's not the fault of the majority of Muslims, they didn't want this any more than the Buddhists did. But it's the Muslim radicals who have finally made it happen. All good liberals blame the Thai government, they blame Thaksin for his mishandling of the war, the excesses, the army's brutality—and they have a point. But ultimately they are kidding themselves. The army will take over in Thailand very soon, and their head is actually a Muslim, and they will depose Thaksin and offer conciliation to the jihadists. But at that point, there will be a huge escalation of violence. The Muslim insurrection— because that's what it is—will have created a military junta in Bangkok and a widening war of atrocity in the south. Make no mistake, they are not seeking respect from any-one, as many have claimed. You don't go around beheading people to get respect. They want secession. I have noticed, everywhere I go, that sizable populations of Muslims will never agree to live under the rule of non-Muslims. Pattani here is going to be just like Mindaloa in the Philippines, Kashmir, Chechnya, Kosovo, you name it. There'll be bombs

in Bangkok soon enough. And look what they did to Bali—
they destroyed its economy."

"Well, well," McGinnis sighed, "how absolutely charming."

"They are going to offer them Sharia law in the South.
And they will reject the offer in favor of more violence."

"I needn't remind you that Sharia law will close down all
the tourism in the South. Our little paradise is going to
shrink."

"What," said McGinnis, aghast, "if they put a bomb in
the Eden Club?"

"My theory is that we thought we would be escaping
to a secure, stable, pleasure-giving, pleasure-loving, lotus-
eating asylum, and instead we have found ourselves stranded
on the fault line between two hostile worlds who will be
struggling over the basic things. Thailand is a secular democ-
racy being hacked at by a theocratic movement which
loathes everything it stands for—and which, I am bound to
add, are the very things we have moved here to embrace.
Naturally, they will kill us without even thinking twice.
Nobody will much care, because they will reason, as cow-
ards always do, that we are perverts and the religious nutters
had a point. But perverts on Monday, little old ladies on
Tuesday, I say."

He asked us if we knew Rumi. Then he quoted something magnificent from that poet:

> *If you pretend to be Hallaj*
> *And with that fake burning*
> *Set fire to your friends,*
> *Don't think that you're a lover.*

You're crazy and numb,
You're drinking our blood,
And you have no experience
Of the nearness.

A crisis later erupted in Islamabad, in Pakistan, when Islamic radicals kidnapped six Chinese businessmen from an upscale massage parlor. The Pakistani army had been forced to surround a mosque, Waco-style, and declare internal war on the group, who clearly had no experience of the nearness. How long, then, before something similar happened in the Land of Smiles?

"I am not a pervert," McGinnis intoned.

•

The next morning I got up early and went up to the outdoor buffet overlooking the rose-petal pool. The skies had darkened even farther. Far out at sea a cloud seemed to be melting downward into the horizon in the shape of a tornado. The staff were watching it with expressions of exasperated incredulity. The end of the world, in all likelihood. It was certainly a dour idea that we were on the front line of the War on Pleasure which would shortly be unleashed upon us. Would we be its unwilling martyrs? But we were certainly here to *experience the nearness.* I smiled and ordered a Continental No-Fat Breakfast with soy croissants and sugarless qumquat jam.

There were racks of newspapers from around the world which clearly no one ever read, the *Corriere della Sera* oddly mixed up with the trash Brit tabloids. I picked out yesterday's *Sun* and had a peep at the page 3 tits before flicking through the usual tales of horror and miscreance from around the world. There was a picture of a stray dog picked up in an estuary in the French island of Réunion with a double-barbed fish hook pushed through its nose. The noble fishermen of that island paradise used stray dogs as live bait for shark fishing, but sometimes the animals escaped from the predators and swam to shore with the hooks through their muzzles. So there's a heartwarming tale about human nature as it really is. The *Sun* called for the fishermen to be executed in public. A reasonable response. I dug into my organic grapefruit.

The manager appeared, a controlled European guy in a severe black suit, a typical European manager's suit with a hangman's tie. He must have been sweating like a pig in that humidity but was at pains not to show it, though anxious beads burst upon his tight, tanned brow. The only guest, eating a grapefruit—he swept up to inspect.

"It's a full-scale hurricane," he sighed. "We are going to close the windows soon with metal storm shutters. We will give you a refunded discount, of course."

"That really isn't necessary," I drawled. Unable to help myself, I put on a Somerset Maugham accent. "Though it's awfully kind of you. I thought there were never storms in November."

"Never. It's a freak."

"Thanks for the kindness anyway."

"It is our pleasure. Excellent grapefruit, no? They are from an organic microfarm in Switzerland."

"A micro—?"

But I stopped; he might just try and explain it.

"A hurricane," I muttered instead. "What a drag."

"What if we all died?" he laughed. A Swiss laugh.

"We have to die sometime. Where better than here?"

"Ah, monsieur, you are a *philosophe*."

I showed him the mutilated dog. "No, monsieur, these are *philosophes*."

"*Quel misère,*" he sighed.

"Organic dog meat. It might be an idea."

Ignoring this, he fingered his tie and bent down a little.

"Monsieur, are you traveling with two other men and a girl?" I said that I was. "Ah. I was just wondering."

"Why?"

"Well, it is just that they are asleep in the water suites. They have been there all night. I don't know how it could have happened."

"How disgusting. Shall I wake them up?"

"No, no. The staff are seeing to it. I thought perhaps you had had a celebration last night."

"Just a bit of rum," I thought. "With a spliff."

His back, as he walked away, glistened with a kind of colonial unhappiness. Suit and tie to keep the natives respectful, and all that. Very soon, the metal shutters began to crank down.

Perversely, I took my coffee outside and sat in the maelstrom quite happily. It was unbearably hot, so the violent winds were not as intimidating as they might have been. The beach looked magnificent and raw, the Hyatt resort next door thrown into hilarious crisis by the battering of its eighty-year-old nut trees. A dog suddenly ran across the beach helter-skelter, its tongue hanging out with joy. Screw the humans, it was thinking—they'll soon be reduced to beggary, like me.

I got up and clambered over the wall down to a long

sand ditch filled with water. A uniformed guard tried politely to stop me, then saluted awkwardly. A guest is a guest. I dropped onto the hard sand and walked up toward the mutilated pistachio trees of the Hyatt. I then ducked into the Hyatt gardens, where the winds had wrought havoc. Their well-heeled guests had obviously all fled back to the capital, leaving the place in the hands of its bewildered staff. In the Polynesian Grill, a chef in a preposterous toque stood flipping burgers with a raging sea as backdrop. I sat by the window and got a Mai Tai. My 9:30 a.m. Mai Tai.

As I was sitting there I saw a familiar figure walking onto the beach from Chiva Som. Fon came over to the Hyatt wall nonchalantly, looked over and saw me, and walked in. She came to my table and sat down, handling her own body with expertise. She looked suavely groomed, as if she had spent far too much time on it, and the wind appeared not to have ruffled any of the thousand invisible feathers that held her image in place. The eyes sparkled; the hands were white as some delicate pork fat. She looked swiftly around, and it was always as if she was doing a visual sweep for attractive men. The pupils inside those eyes sharpened like pencil points, sheer black acidic lead. She had the unmistakable look of a woman looking for a missing husband, lover, or gold mine. But I have never held that against anyone, and to accuse women of gold-digging is surely to miss the point in the context of an arrangement where the man is several times richer than the woman, through no one's fault. And the men, just as invariably, wearily accept the terms of the arrangement. Money is just money. But sexual companionship is priceless. Lionel was the source of her Californian jewelry.

"So there you are," she said at once, swinging slightly

wet hair. "At least you're not drunk like those two. Oh, they bad men. Make me want cry. Old, silly men. You nice young man, you not marry and here you are."

"Yes, here I am."

She made for a smooth coquette.

"We have little time. You want go in Hyatt?"

"I think Lionel might be a little hurt." Now I was curious. "Do you love him, Fon? No, really."

But she knew it was a sentimental question. Perhaps love is a rare lightning that strikes only one in ten of the population. Her foot touched mine under the table and she looked mock-hurt. Why not make an extra bit on the side while the French bastard was asleep in the water suites?

"I love Lio," she said slowly. "He's bad bad man, but he is kind as well."

"But don't you want a family, children?"

"With Lio?"

"With whoever."

It's a cruel question at the best of times. Fon was the daughter of a shrimp fisherman in Phang Nga. Eight children, no money from the shrimp business, and the prospect only of marriage to another shrimp fisherman followed by a life of respectable drudgery. She must have looked at her mother and decided not to go that route. It's a classic story.

For a hundred years and more the world's fast-developing cities have been filled with ambitious, fearful, gutsy young girls striking out with the odds stacked against them in search of an escape from what their backgrounds have prepared for them.

In Bangkok they were already almost half the workforce across the board. If you got your teeth done there, as I did, you quickly noticed that in dentistry they were predominant. The same was apparently true in biotechnology and countless service sectors. Sukhumvit Road at eight in the morning is not filled with bar girls, it's filled with streams of women in business suits on their way to work. NGOs have long pretended that a tenth of the female population is engaged in sex work, but the obvious falsity of this has recently been exposed. Instead, the relation of sex work to normal work has been stranger. As Thailand has become richer, the sex business has actually expanded, in contrast to the usual experience of industrializing countries, such as Japan. Thai sociologists scratch their heads over it. They theorize that in a society with a pliable sense of sexual morality, sex can easily be seen as just another economic weapon to get ahead. The trade fills with part-timers who use it, for example, to save up enough to make a down payment on an apartment.

She had met Lionel at some foamy nightclub like Q Bar, seen at once the advantages he offered, and then latched on to him like a remora fish. It was mutual predation. What did Fon want? Not a foreign john, but a foreign husband who would take her away. Such stories are legion in the bar-girl world. The grapevines of gossip hum like telephone cables at peak time, and no upwardly mobile girl is going to turn a deaf ear to them when she knows her chances are small in number and have to be exploited to the maximum. And there are her fears, of old age, of poverty. But these are everyone's fears.

She picked her teeth skeptically.

"You are not married either," she retorted. "That's why you come Thai girl. We know, we know." And then a smile as brilliant as candy.

"Lionel will never marry you," I wanted to warn her. "He's an incorrigible libertine." But, then again, I didn't know. Libertines are lonely creatures, and they too slip the ring eventually. Fon, moreover, was patient.

•

After lunch, I went to the water suites. Behind a large indoor pool there are corridors of water with pebbles underfoot, along which guests in towels can venture. There are recesses, fountains, dim-lit steam rooms, all the atmosphere of a Roman bath, but no sign of my companions. The day went to waste, and that is the point of a spa: to waste time. The water suites were perhaps the least interesting thing in Hua Hin, and yet here was where the Westerners with the most money spent much of their time. Clearly, people enjoy their own sterility.

At five, said companions appeared, smoking cigars which an anguished attendant immediately rushed to extinguish. There was a tussle as the damp stubs were thrown about in confusion like toxic waste.

"A Cuesta-Rey for nothing!" I heard McGinnis shout.

Health experts appeared in white coats, crying foul. So in the first mellow hour of evening, we took a *tuk tuk* into town to escape the stifling morality of the spa. Downtown Hua Hin was a small, simple place with a boisterous night market, plenty of hookers, and some mouth-searing food. There was a tiny beach sandwiched between buildings. Small restaurants bubbled away on the wooden decks.

Eventually we got a table and the women brought over sheaves of lemongrass, dark-red sauces in glass bottles, wedges of lemon and mint, dainty saucers of tangy *naam phrik plaa*. A wave hit the window full square and there was a bout of merry screaming—or not quite so merry. We ordered the carp and a sea bass and Singha beers. McGinnis and Lionel were in high spirits, and Fon watched them both with a glass-eyed curiosity which was easily persuaded to turn to laughter. If you can't make a Thai laugh you're a dead fish.

Without warning, I felt an intense love for the three out-casts, who were not so much swimming their way through life as drowning with a show of bravado. The signs of bravado were moving: Lionel's dyed and probably implanted hair, a shockingly crude camel color now with weird-looking roots showing through; the disgusting pommade in McGin-nis's hair which cast an aromatic spell around him, a smell of decayed vegetables and a sweetshop in hundred-degree heat; his eye that moved and gleamed like a mackerel; the hopeless earnestness of Fon's hair, which didn't move even in that wind. She now lit up like a Christmas light, like a female Santa made of hot glass, and all her striving and ruthlessness came into her face, and her bumptious, delicious animality rose as she drank and lost control. She told Lionel to go fuck himself and went through a bottle of rice whiskey, at the bot-tom of which lurked a small embalmed scorpion. It was a present from McGinnis, who called it "scorpion vodka." The drinkers of Southeast Asia are fond of placing snakes and venomous insects inside bottles of rice wine and whis-key, and the scorpion whiskeys have a distinctive peaty after-taste that mitigates the cheap astringency of the drink itself.

"As a matter of fact," McGinnis said, tilting the bottle at me, "they leach the venom out of them first. What is left is pure thrill."

The custom among hard drinkers is to empty the bottle and then eat the soggy disarmed *Heterometrus spinifer*. For men weaned on "express trains" and fried waterbugs, it is hardly an insurmountable ordeal.

"I had a banana-flavored scorpion liqueur once," Lionel observed mildly. "I threw up for a day and a night, but I ate the fucker. It tasted like a banana crêpe."

"We had it together," the girl said. "You say Thai disgusting people, drink that stuff with claw. I say, cheer, and we drink this scorpi vodka."

McGinnis leaned to my ear.

"They can't drink, you know. Listen to her disintegrating English. Delightful to listen to."

"I don't remember you drinking the banana one, darling. Are you sure?"

"Banana scorpion *and* ice-blue melon."

"Well, cheers," McGinnis cried, and tipped the *Heterometrus* sideways so that its two claws rolled against the glass bottle as if it was waving at us. "Last one to finish eats the *bestiole*!"

Fon: "Me, me! You pussy *farang*. Only Thai woman can eat."

She tossed off a glass, then another.

"She's not an alcoholic," Lionel explained mildly. "She just gets these drinking fits. She's like an express train that can't stop."

When Thais drink, all hell often breaks loose. When Thai women drink, there is an extraordinary unraveling which happens in the blink of an eye. The façade of *riab roi*, of respectable demeanor, suddenly cracks and gives way, and a torrent of buried passion often comes cascading out through portals that were hitherto unimagined. They collapse, dance on tables, cry, whirl about like tops, and fall asleep quickly. The sexuality that plays subtly across their sober surface, so devastating because it is so understated and reserved, so aware of itself at the deepest level—aware, that is, of the ultimate consequences—is now broken up into confessions, scenes, and slippages.

Fon upended the empty bottle and out came the scorpion. She cut it up with a fork while Lionel looked on with a great bead of sweat between his eyebrows.

"Now, now, *chérie*. That's really not necessary."

But she was on a roll and soon the legs, the thorax, and, finally, the claws were going down her gullet.

"It's really quite magnificent," McGinnis was moved to comment. *"Voilà la femme thai."* His glance to Lionel was eloquent: You want to marry this scorpion-quaffing warrior?

"You'll be up all night," Lionel sighed.

"Make me horny, yes."

For the scorpion, like the cobra, when added to these "wines" is reputed to be an aphrodisiac.

I was feeling horny myself after a half-shot of the brew. Would Lionel chivalrously offer a four-way orgy, or a three-way at least? It didn't seem likely. And so my attention drifted out to sea, where buoys and little shrimp boats tossed about in the winds. Someone had told me that this coastline was once devoted to the profitable cultivation of walnuts (I have no idea if that is true) but that the nut farmers had long ago discovered that it was more profitable to work at the Hilton and the Hyatt than it was to prune nut trees. So the nut groves had withered and the coast had turned inexorably into a tourist installation.

•

On Monday morning our driver emerged from the dawn in his gray buttoned gloves (where had he been all weekend?)

and *wai*'ed, as did the Chiva Som staff who saw us off. They apologized for the atrocious weather, as if weather could be apologized for.

"Well, let's get back to where we belong," Lionel said to the driver when we were in the car, the rain drumming on the roof.

And soon we were among the rice paddies again, and the cranky windmills turning clockwise, dripping lethargic water. We said nothing all the way back to Bangkok. The land became more definite as we sped farther from Hua Hin, which seemed to be suffering from a local downpour, and we could see the farms laid out against the lines of rice, and the children swimming in rancid puddles as the buffalo looked on, lost no doubt in their very boring vegetarian dreams.

The house appeared to be empty when I got back, and the gardener informed me that Kitty had gone to her country house to supervise a new batch of sick dogs from the rural monasteries there. At night, the garden lamps were left off as Kitty's fear of the dark was not in play, and under the influence of the last of the epiglottitis drugs I had several mystical episodes during which I saw Kitty's aunt and uncle walking across the lawns in the early hours with their teapot and pruning shears. "Mysticism," wrote Max Nordau, "is the expression of the inaptitude for attention, for clear thought and control of the emotions, and has for its cause the weakness of the higher cerebral centers." Hear, hear, Max, but I saw them all the same. It occurred to me that hallucinations are not difficult to create in the system of someone taking drug cocktails, but all the same, I was surprised at how clear and definite the old couple looked as they inspected the mango trees they had planted themselves during the Second World War. It was now that I realized that although the main house was all new, the plot itself might have belonged to the family for a century, and the warehouses behind my garden could easily have been from the 1940s. It was a period that no one ever talked about, in contrast to Anglo-American culture, where the forties are talked about incessantly. It had never occurred to me to ask why. Why this haste to cover up even the recent past?

It so happened that my follow-up examinations and checkups were assigned to a doctor at the Mongkutklao Hospital, a man named Daemkern, and for a few weeks we became quite friendly, as doctor and patient sometimes do. Neither Thais nor foreigners take much interest in the secluded and accidentally preserved fragments of the last hundred years, which lie scattered about the metropolis. A train station here, a library there. It is as if a great event called "modernity" occurred like a natural disaster of some kind, severing the present from the past, which could be located, for the sake of argument, prior to 1965 or so. Few are the men or women who are haunted by this fact, but Daemkern was one of them, and this was an ample platform upon which to construct many conversations. Like most educated Thais, his English was as good as mine. He was boyishly curious about why I was spending so much time in Bangkok when it was obvious I didn't have a job there and I didn't need to be there. When I explained to him that I was on the lam, he laughed as if he understood this to mean that I was running away from my wife—like taking a yacht and secretly going round the world on it with a stash of caviar and Viagra. My fuller explanations made little sense to him, and he would nod and nod and look at his nails. There was a picture on his wall of a ten-year-old daughter in a smock standing next to a plastic marlin suspended from a chain. There was an amber paperweight with a wasp entombed inside. His wife, he said, had bought it at the Tucson Gem Show.

"There is a palace hidden on the hospital grounds," he said during the first visit. "It's a short walk from here. If you like, since you seem to be curious about such things, I could take you around. I have a lunch break. Perhaps next time. It's called the Pyathai. It's not open to the public, so I'll have to take you around."

He took my pulse and blood pressure and observed that I seemed abnormally anxious in some way.

"Or is that the way you usually are?"

•

The King Mongkutklao Hospital stands on a wide street called Ratchawithi, and the hospital itself is something of a mini-city spread over many grimy acres. For forty minutes I would sit in a traffic jam in which I was able to learn the Thai word for this phenomenon from every driver whose dashboard reeked with little Buddhas, some of which lit up and emitted electronic laughs. *Rot-din gern.* "Traffic too much."

Ratchawithi boils with traffic, its sidewalks are broken, its trees reduced to shreds. Pedestrians scramble across its lanes with a kind of acrobatic panic. I would arrive sweating and stifled.

On my second visit, Daemkern asked me what I thought of the hospital. It is tricky, however, to both entertain an opinion about a hospital in someone else's country and to express it to the face of someone who spends half his life in it. Daemkern was about fifty-five, stocky, and pockmarked, and his was one of those male physiques which are actually improved by such a blemish. It made him look like a swarthy tough. If he had whipped out a switchblade as he examined my throat I wouldn't have been surprised. He had a silver cigarette case with a kanji character on the lid. I've never trusted a doctor who doesn't smoke.

The Pyathai lies on its own grounds to one side of the main hospital. From the road there appears a gate of stained Corinthian columns, a cluster of red gothic spires, and a balustraded bridge of some kind. The roofs could have been copied from the skyline of Dijon, but on a smaller scale. It is not announced by any obvious sign, but as part of a working hospital I suppose it wouldn't be.

It was hot now, one in the afternoon, the sun strong and unremitting. Daemkern put on his shades and walked with the gait of a golfer. We strolled past an old howitzer and a gray pavilion with painted eaves, vaguely Ottoman in feel. Behind this stood a fountain sculpture of a large swan being grappled by two boys. It looked as if the swan was being throttled by one of them, while the other blew a trumpet. Daemkern let out a pert laugh. Victorian frippery of the sort that elites all over the world indulged in a hundred years ago: the style of an insecure Asian monarchy in an age of other people's empires. And there one senses the unease. The era when Siam was at the mercy of Europeans—not their gunboats but their awful taste.

To the right rose the main building, a former royal palace built by King Rama V in the 1890s and once a great hotel. To the left stood a separate pavilion, now a teahouse. On the steps of the hospital a few nurses sat smoking cigarettes. There were patients, too, people in wheelchairs sipping sodas, a child with a bandaged eye staring at the foreigner making his way to the palace, a man with burnished skin the color and texture of a primate's fingers.

We went into the pavilion tearoom through cool teak doors, the vaults in Art Deco style. The teahouse was octagonal in shape; a group of old ladies sat around one table

with pots of Earl Grey. The dark wood and herringbone par-
quet were suddenly soothing and Daemkern and I sat as if
exhausted, the sweat cooling on our faces. The Deco ceilings
loomed above window casements with all their original
brass locks: there were gold lamps with frosted shades, pan-
eling with tropical fruit carved in miniature. Vases of fabric
flowers had vertiginous little bird's nests loopily popping
out. In one corner, very incongruous, stood an ice cream
freezer straight out of a British seaside town. Through the
stained-glass windows came the green heat of the park, the
coo of pigeons.

Daemkern glanced over at the biddies and ordered Earl
Grey for us, too. His mood was chipper—but when was it
not?

"Rama VI lived here, too, you know, and I daresay he
was our most curious king. Nineteen ten to nineteen twenty-
five. A curious period in Asia. This palace is where he tried
to create a utopian model society called Dusit Thani, with its
own newspapers and currency. It was sort of mad, naturally,
but I have always had a soft spot for him. He was whimsical
and literary. He introduced the spoken Western play into
Thailand—did you know that? Though of course nobody
today has any interest in spoken literary plays. Or in him,
for that matter."

"It's a shame."

"We are not a very history-minded people. Or we
haven't been up to now. At least they have restored this
pavilion."

"They have done it rather well."

"I confess it's my favorite tearoom. My wife and I come
here sometimes to have a quiet talk."

"It's strange," I said. "But it feels like a time warp. One doesn't feel that in the big temples, the palaces the tourists go to, even though they are much older. Those places somehow never feel old. Wat Po doesn't feel old to me. It feels like something that was built yesterday."

"I have felt the same thing. It's strange indeed, isn't it?"

I said, "Perhaps the reason you don't make such a fuss over the past is simply because in reality it doesn't exist. It's an idea, nothing more. And ideas are soap bubbles. Of course, you could say that architecture isn't a soap bubble."

"It's funny. I go to the morgue twice a week and I see all these dead bodies. Are people like soap bubbles, too?"

"It depends if one is a doctor or not."

"Or a Buddhist. Everything transient and all that."

This relatively recent room felt ancient precisely because it was largely forgotten. Buildings are the great mysteries of our lives.

"My grandfather," Daemkern went on, "used to say the loveliest palace in Bangkok was the Wang Burapha. I always wanted to see it, but for some unknown reason it was demolished just after the war and replaced by the Grand and King's Cinema. When you look at photographs of it, you are amazed by its size and complexity. A building of such grandness and solidity—destroyed in a single week. And replaced by what? A cinema!"

•

We wandered over to the main building. A canal stood by some blue wooden pavilions, and we went up an empty staircase next to the Army Corps Medical Museum. The second floor looked more like a hospital, voices sweeping down

immense galleries of dimmed frescoes, with paper chandeliers hanging in hot shade.

In mold-tinted air, breathing comes a little harder. The
windows were gaping holes without glass; echoes rolled
down the galleries, around which vestiges of paint still clung
to the upper parts of the walls: forests slowly receded into
oblivion. Their palms and vines offered a vision of un-
planted abundance, a Thai Garden of Eden. The forest,
which seems to exist always in the Thai subconscious.

We strolled through those galleries which formed a
maze, with rectangular detours and corners of grandiosity.
The fire extinguishers had probably not been used since
before my birth. One passageway was a covered bridge leading to more of the palace. It seemed to me that this upper
part of the building had not been used much since the mid-
century, not even as a luxury hotel, that something had
brought its social functionality to a halt.

"I don't know the exact history of it," he admitted. "I
don't even know why they stopped using it as a hotel. It just
seemed old-fashioned at some point. It must have been
that."

"I am curious. Do you ever think about the war period?
I never hear it mentioned. There are scores of big-budget his-
torical movies about the sixteenth and seventeenth centuries,
blockbusters like *Sukhothai*, which Thais seem to love, and
yet nothing about the Second World War. Is the sixteenth
century really more interesting to the mass market than the
last war?"

"Less shameful, is the answer to that. The Second World
War was an awkward period for Thailand."

He said that you could argue it different ways. The

absolute monarchy was ended in 1932 by a coup of army
officers, one of the most prominent of whom had been a
man called Luang Phibunsongkram. But the monarchy was
impossible to extirpate. This was no England 1649, or
France 1789. The army had been frustrated by what they
saw as the nation's backwardness relative to the great pow-
ers of Europe. The striking Europeanization of the monarchs
themselves was not the issue. They looked to Fascist Italy as
a way out of inferiority, out of commercial and cultural sub-
ordination. Modernize, modernize. Outstrip the West. Inter-
nalize technological habits. It had had a curious effect upon
them, he said. They were archaic and postmodern at the
same time.

Phibunsongkram became one of the least known but
most successful dictators of the twentieth century. He took
power first in 1938, was deposed in 1944, and then staged a
remarkable political comeback in 1948, ruling until 1957,
when he was deposed a second time after rigging dirty elec-
tions and mishandling a drought in the north. One could say
that the whole period between 1932 and 1957 was dominated by the military and by Phibun, as he was known. It
was he who imposed the name "Thailand," replacing the
older and lovelier "Siam."

Phibun was Thailand's Marshal Pétain. The country was
occupied by the Japanese after suffering a brief invasion, but
under his dictatorship she engineered a masterly surrender
and compliance. The country was never a wartime Japanese
colony in name; in practice, she was more like Vichy.

Under Phibun, a program of cultural nationalism was
undertaken between 1938 and 1944. The name of the country was changed, the Chinese were put in their place, and

Thais for the first time were forced by law to wear Western dress. A bizarre system of personal regulation was set up, with citizens forbidden to board buses or to pay their taxes at government offices bareheaded. Twelve Cultural Mandates were passed, aimed at making Thais modern. The Western calendar was imposed, and Luang Wichit, the regime's chief propagandist, wrote that since the Chinese were comparable to the Jews of Germany, the same methods as Hitler's might be used against them.

As the Japanese closed in, Phibun invaded Laos and Cambodia to recover provinces stolen from Siam by the French. As the calendar, the hat, and the clock were imposed, the government's slogan became "Thailand for the Thais!" just as the Thais became less Thai than ever. And just as Vichy gave birth to contemporary France, though few would like to admit it, so Phibun's Thailand gave rise to the nation around us now. Like all Western countries, it was forcibly wedded to the idea of progress, which was never defined or imagined except vaguely, as something that moves forward with such pitiless force that it can clothe itself with the adjective "inevitable."

What did any of this have to do with the Pyathai? Nothing directly. But it did have something to do with the forgetting, with hasty burials. With amnesia and oblivion, or merely with carelessness.

We followed the corridors until we came to a room filled with jolly portraits of King Bhumipol, the current incumbent on the Thai throne. By the doors there was a spacious patio like that of a colonial hotel, where the trees came close, spilling their humidity. It used to be a pleasure palace, a fin-de-siècle folly. There must have been costume parties, masked balls, ambassadorial receptions, flirtations of the upper class: but now the ceilings gaped with holes, were streaked with fungus. Daemkern was right. The city had little interest in its own past.

An oily gloom washed across me as we pushed open a door where we were not supposed to go. It was a secretive little reception room with ten identical doors, and from the ceiling lamps trailed bizarre glass tassels like crystal jellyfish. We stepped inside and closed the door behind us. It was a hundred degrees inside. There was Rama VI again on a back wall, in his red silk suit, round-faced, melancholy and sympathetic, his hands folded in front of him, watching me with a birdy eye. A character out of Velázquez. So here was the man who had introduced the spoken Western play to Thailand, and did anyone go to spoken plays these days? Hardly anyone, I would imagine. And why had the utopian idea of Dusit Thani, the ideal city, not caught on? Because nobody wants to live inside a utopia? And because nobody trusts an eccentric king?

One night I got out at the Siam Skytrain station, where the "permanent demonstration" against the government was taking place. It was a party scene. Thousands of squatters were assembled under the Skytrain tracks across from the Paragon Mall, and as I exited the train with hundreds of students, pink balloons imprinted with the words *Evil of Thailand* closed in around me, along with red flags with an image of a mounted knight, a Thai Don Quixote, whose meaning escaped me. I went down to the street, between ad panels for Black Canyon Coffee and Pizza Hut. I sailed by a poster for a popular sorbet, a maid's strawberry face and the words *Good Time Good Feeling*. I bought a "Thaksin Devil" pin, stuck it in my shirt, and wandered through this doomed orgy. There's no point protesting globalism when you are sitting in its lap. Or perhaps that's all you can do.

After listening to some hysterical speeches, I pushed through the mass to the commercial square beneath the Paragon Mall. I was not alone in the mall's glass atrium lobby, which is made bold by towering palms and waterfalls. Many participants in the demonstrations were also walking across the square to take a break inside the air-conditioned mall. On the ground floor, the Peninsula Café was full, the golf ball sets and teddy bears looking as if they might become animate at any moment, and there the exhausted demonstrators sat with tall iced coffees and green teas, exuding not the slightest hostility toward their surroundings. But

why did I myself feel blind here, where the light was so daz-
zling, among the rocking horses, gemstones, garden furniture, and golfing slacks?

In the basement mall metal water lilies rose from the
ornamental ponds. There was a sound of water everywhere.
On the ground floor stood a Pilates light aircraft for sale,
around which a pensive Thai businessman was pacing as if
considering buying it. What a way to spend one's evening—
contemplating an aircraft purchase on the ground floor of a
mall. A demonstration against globalization on one side of
the square, a guy pondering a Pilates aircraft on the other. It
seems to prove that demonstrations are a leftover of the
nineteenth century.

I went down to the Aquarium and wandered through
glittering sea horses and baby sharks. Then upstairs again to
a Lifestyle Gallery, where rows of cars were on sale. There
were many "halls"—a Hall of Mirrors, a Hall of Fame.
There was even a section named "World Class Brand Name"
and a "Lifestyle and Leisure" floor. There were demonstrators here, too, taking a break: in Bang & Olufsen, the sales-
girls stood stock-still, like funeral attendants awaiting their
demise. The great galleries began to empty; on a wall, a garland of giant mock jewels and the golden word *Bulgari*
began to fade as the lights were lowered a little and the tropical plants on either side of the ceremonial elevators took on
a wilting sadness. I went to the floor where Thai antiques
shops were arrayed, places like Exotique Thai and Bellitas,
and sat on a bench in the Panyin Passage. Two women
played a *ranaat eek* in the ghostly emptiness.

•

"Personally," Dennis said later that night when we met up, "I cannot see why anyone would demonstrate for or against something unless it were under a dictatorship. Only dictatorships are worried by demonstrations. Businessmen, mate, don't give a hoot about them. And democracies are run by businessmen and managers."

"I don't mind being run by managers," I grumbled as we came out of Somboon's on Ratchada. "Not some of the time, anyway. You know what they say. Efficiency liberates."

"When I was running the bank back in Perth, that was my motto. Now I think efficiency fucks you up."

"Anyway, the demo was fun. The middle classes going beserk."

"Mate, I can't think of anything worse than the middle classes going berserk. They are berserk all the time, aren't they?"

It was time for one of our famous walks, and we set off into a toxic dusk. Down tough backstreets which intersected in a curvilinear way, to a large urban temple with bloodred gates and a turquoise wat which I had been visiting for a few months.

Surrounded by filthy canals and tin shacks, there was a long mural of Buddha sitting under his tree, as beautifully crude as something painted by children. I never knew what this temple was called, or why tattooed slum kids played soccer in its lovely vanilla courtyards. It was just there, and it was available. The surrounding neighborhood felt like an ancient village. The nearest street I could identify was Pracha Songkhro, and the neighborhood, as I perhaps wrongly understood it, was Huai Khwang.

"I like it here," Dennis wheezed as he shuffled along,

and I thought sadly that he looked indescribably shabby and old now, as if time had not only caught up with him but roughed him up in the process. "I sometimes come to Huai Khwang just to look at the youth. It feels like another city."

He walked with his stick, leaning heavily on it and keeling leftward with each step. The handle was carved in the shape of a duck's head. He had recently been back to Perth to sell his house and now lived full-time in Bangkok. He wouldn't buy anything here, though, because he'd have no one to leave it to.

"I'll be forgotten as soon as I die. Here you just melt away and it's like you never existed. This just encourages you to live in the present as much as you can. No worries."

The sky has a neon tinge here, soft and elastic. The clotheslines draped all over the tenements look like Buddhist prayer flags fluttering around a stone outcrop in Tibet. They are real slum streets, chattering and gossipy, filled with little plant pots, smoked out with incense and furious woks.

Dennis shook and flipped like a dried leaf, grinning at his own ridiculous frailty. He wore a crumpled straw hat, made in China of course, and its cheapo satin band had crumpled as well, like something worn in a bedroom night in and night out. He was crablike in his movements, probing surfaces with stick and foot, and sometimes hand, as if he were inching his way along a rock face upside down, defying the laws of gravity. All the while his eyes popped and slithered left and right as if considerable dangers lurked around every corner. I found myself helping him along, and as I did so, quiet tears came into my eyes and I had to subdue them because there was nothing that pithy Dennis hated more than a masculine tear, especially one being shed at his expense. Instead, he played Old Man, lifting his stick to point out curious details in the streets. A woman beating her husband with a newspaper on a distant balcony; two cats copulating by the side of a half-buried canal traversed by planks. A woman with a portable grill and bundles of eggs thrown over her shoulder.

"Water, water," he murmured, "the whole place is made of water, built on water. Like life. Life is nearly all water, not stone."

That night I was in Ratchada because Dennis had invited me to one of his card games which were held sometimes at the Swissotel. For years he had been excessively secretive about the card games he reputedly played with a circle of *farang* and Thai old-timers, one of whom was a retired Thai colonel of some notoriety whose name, like Beelzebub's, could not be uttered lest lightning strike you. People like McGinnis thought that Dennis made most of his "spare cash" playing in these poker games, because of course bank managers are good with figures and are rumored to make excellent card players. They can hold their own with anyone. I, on the other hand, was probably the shittiest card player in Asia. I could be beat by anyone, and to boot I was, as always, broke. No matter, said Dennis. He'd stump me the money to play a few hands. And, he added, I had to see the Swissotel, it was the most vulgar hotel on earth, outside of Malaysia. It was so vulgar it made your head spin; it made you sweat on a cold day. It was so vulgar there was nowhere else to play the Wednesday-night game.

"And you?" he asked as we painfully made our way back to Ratchada and looked, through all-submersing traffic, for the butch outline of the Swissotel. "Are you in love yet? Married? Seeking?"

"I am waiting in the wings."

"You have that about you, mate: a waiter in wings. You'd better step out soon. No one gets any younger."

"One doesn't necessarily get older, either."

"Ha, a man after my own heart."

•

The Swissotel Concorde is a remarkable place. So vulgar that almost as soon as you enter it you begin to feel intoxicated, assaulted by fairies, carried away by some mysterious force of which only the purveyors of extreme vulgarity are the custodians. At the door stood a footman in a tall white top hat and white gloves. For a second, he could have been mistaken for a giant rabbit.

Inside, you are in a business hotel exhibiting a certain restraint. There's a fairly normal lobby with fairly normal-looking suits. Look up, however, and you see that you are under a vast cupola copied with some license—but almost exactly—from the Sistine Chapel. Adam, God, outstretched hands, the ignition point of evolution: it's all there. All right, that's not so bad. You've seen worse. But there is something about the scale of the thing. It's the monumental black columns that surround it and the chandelier from hell that drops down from the middle of it. Your eyes bulge and ache. You know this is European bad taste, not the Asian variety. This is the sort of thing the Mitteleuropean entrepreneur class would love to build in Europe if they could get the permits and the space. Dennis looked up, squinted, and laughed.

"It bears all the hallmarks of our old friend Helix. He's still around, you know. And this is exactly the kind of *mierda* he likes to paint."

Subtending to this funeral parlor is an equally outsized dining room, which hosts one of the city's more cavernous buffets. Men in puffy toques stand around ready to explain the dubious contents of the metal containers around which a motley crowd of international types fuss like hesitant birds. The walls are fleshed out with long, detailed frescoes detailing many scenes from the life of ancient Greece. A view of mountains that suggest Delphi on a fine day, girls in flowing chitons, sandaled ephebes in greaves and garlands. A sound of fountains and a great pentagonal lamp with copper leaves sprouting from it. One of the most curious things about Bangkok is the way that Greco-Roman motifs are freely used to varnish buildings with an aura of power and respectability. The content of these motifs is not really known, but *satai roman* is so widely used by the rich, by developers, and by the aspirant middle classes that one has to conclude that they see something in Greece and Rome that they want to associate with. The entertainment palace next door to the Swissotel is called Caesar's.

In one corner of this pseudo-palatial room sat the card cabal, five older men in light summer shirts eating from plates of pork satay. They were all *farang* except for a mottled old Thai with an eye patch. He was "Mr. S."

What followed was odd, to say the least. A scene from Gombrowicz, the writer I found myself reading and rereading and devouring afresh in Bangkok—the supreme artist of exile. The seven of us seemed to know each other, and yet we did not know each other. I thought we would be playing for money, but in fact there was no money on the table at all. There were merely notepads and seven pens. The *farang*s were paunchy and mottled, too, men who had been here since the seventies. One of them was wearing a Marine Corps beret, class of '44, and another had laid a pair of crutches against the wall. They hurled little pellets of comradely sarcasm at the late arrival, and I saw now with some surprise that Dennis had a social life after all, that he was somewhat less lonely than I had assumed him to be.

"You old lecher. Who's the lad?"

"A younger lecher. A lad no more—but looks young for his age, wouldn't you say? Or he might be a hundred for all I know. I picked him up on the street years ago."

"Siddown, then."

The card game is a showdown, a theatrical confrontation which turns its participants into masks who act exactly according to a hidden nature.

"How many numbers do you have?" Mr. S asked in excellent English.

"Numbers?"

"We trade numbers at this table, not money. Did Bob tell you?"

"Bob?"

Dennis winked at me. So here he was Bob.

"Bob," the eye-patched one said. "Does he have a few numbers?"

"Of course he does. He's a *farang* in Bangkok, isn't he? How could he not have numbers? I wouldn't have asked him if he didn't."

It was clear enough what they meant. Each player wrote down a telephone number on a sheet and tendered it as a kind of chip. I groaned inwardly, since apart from the fact that I had no numbers to offer, I saw little point in receiving them, either. Assuming that they were the numbers of night ladies. I played only in order to be close a little longer to Dennis, whom I loved in a way, and whom I always considered to be on the brink of an unnameable disaster from which he would have to be saved. I wrote down all sorts of numbers and "lost" them. They included the local electricity company's hot line, a friend who had moved back to Antwerp, and the press office of the Human Development Agency's Catholic outreach hospice in Klong Tuey. All the while, Dennis chattered away. He was making progress with his painting. He was writing a journal about Bangkok, which would be a unique record of the city at the beginning of the twenty-first century. No one would read it after his death, but no matter. He might donate it to Chulalongkorn University. A course for freshmen in 2050: Farangs in the Bangkok Fin-de-Siècle.

"You're a bloody fool, Bob," someone said with laconic tone. "You should just stick to Q Bar."

•

We played till midnight. The men told their stories for the sake of a newcomer. One of them was a detective who chased down false insurance claims.

"I am not the legendary Byron Bales," the guy said ruefully. "I am Mr. Cling. That's what they call me, Mr. Cling. A nickname is as good as a name in this place."

Cling was about sixty, Canadian, with some sort of paramilitary background. For as Farlo had pointed out, the city was a magnet for ex-military types who couldn't reintegrate back into normal civvie life. It was a fine place for people who missed battlefields.

"I had a guy last month who jumped off a yacht—his

own yacht—off Costa Rica and was presumed drowned.
He'd gone to amazing lengths. Left a wife, a kid, the lot.
They held a funeral in Santa Barbara. He didn't have debts;
he didn't have a motive at all. No mistress, nothing. He just
wanted to disappear. Just for the hell of it. A midlife crisis.
There comes a moment when you've just had enough and
you jump. You might not even know why. Of course, most
of them are after the insurance money."

More common, therefore, was the certificate issued by
the American Embassy called an F-180, the Death of an
American Abroad. Dozens had been filed in recent years,
most of them insurance frauds. The most notorious was the
case of the Kongsiri, a wealthy Thai couple who emigrated
to the U.S., returned to Thailand with a generous policy,
then faked her death to claim it. The embassy rarely checked
the authenticity of death certificates, which were quite easy
to procure in Thailand with a timely *propina*. The city's
detective agencies spent a lot of their time following up these
fraudulent certificates. (In later years I visited the charming
and elusive Byron Bales at his seaside home in Ban Krut, five
hours south of Bangkok. He confirmed these details.)

There was a moment when I had to look over at Dennis.
When it came down to it, I knew nothing about him whatsoever. It was in the nature of the city that one didn't delve
too deeply into a man's background, and even less into a
woman's. Surfaces were all, and surfaces had to be tranquil,
inviolate. His left eye twitched and he smiled. He knew all
about these stories: Bangkok lore.

"The Kongsiri were a Bales case. There's a wonderful
book called *Bangkok Babylon* by Jerry Hopkins where you
can read all about it. The wife went back to the States by

herself, remarried her husband and became, in effect, his second wife. It worked. But then the husband got greedy and decided to pull the stunt in reverse, with himself as the deceased. So they went back to Thailand to do it again. Alas for him, he was spotted at Bangkok airport after his own demise. It gave a whole new meaning to the idea of reincarnation."

When I had lost all my emergency hotline numbers, I nudged my benefactor and Dennis lost no time in extricating us. He was so drunk he had to stagger through the buffet room on the arm of a waiter, and as we passed under the Sistine dome he began to drool onto his shirt. "It's terrible," he muttered as I dabbed him clean. "The muscles in the jaw just go, like elastic bands."

•

We walked aimlessly along Sukhumvit, near Soi 2, then the Landmark, past old haunts that never seemed old. I was going to walk him home to Soi 24, but I could tell there was a reluctance to get to that dismal, claustrophobic destination. There was a queer atmosphere on the street. Military trucks shot by in the direction of Ploenchit. Crowds of protesters caused traffic jams. Near Soi 11 some undercover cops stopped a car with two *kathoey* transvestites. With the police was an enraged Dutchman who had obviously just been robbed in a seedy hotel by the *kathoey*, perhaps posing as Amazonian women. The cops spread-eagled the trannies on the tarmac with guns to their heads while the Dutch wallet was retrieved. The language was too fast; I couldn't catch what the undercovers were hissing at the *kathoey*, but Dennis said, "They're telling them they're worthless scum." No one could have guessed that by the end of the year 2006, Thailand would be ruled by a military junta, an event largely ignored by the Western media, even though the signs were all around us then. Societies are like large tanks of nervous fish. The exile, because he is alert to the tiniest dislocation in his circumambient atmosphere, is sometimes aware of such developments before the locals, who so pride themselves on a suave familiarity with their own culture. Dennis was an antenna of this sort. He knew what was what, and there was a quality of dread in his voice at times. The brilliant shops, the confluence of races, the pursuit of pleasure—they could all be swept away, as indeed they so often were in history. Where was the city through which Petronius's Giton flashed like a minnow? Dennis often said to me that Bangkok reminded him of an ancient Roman city, at least as we imagine them to have been. Cities of polytheistic lust. Nothing, he added, could be further removed from the cities of Anglophonia, which were based not on a love of pleasure but on a worship of power.

"Personally," Dennis said as we reached Soi 24, "I have always hated clean cities. Cities should be as dirty as possible. Dirt is the sign that they are healthy. Not trash—that's something else. We don't want pizza cartons and Big Mac wrappers everywhere. That's obscene. No, I mean decayed fruit and swill and pig bones and spittle. I'm okay with that. General all round sputum. Give me Naples over San Diego any day. Give me Bangkok over any British or American or Australian shithole any day. You know who we are? We're the rancorous old lady standing behind the lace curtain calling the police because we see someone having it off in his own bedroom. Think of how *sentimental* it is. We're mental masturbators without a right hand."

Speaking of pleasures of the body and mind, it was about this time that I introduced myself to Father Joe Maier. It was not because I needed to meet anyone new but because I was simply growing curious about the part of Bangkok in which I was living. Maier ran a Catholic mission in the Klong Tuey slums, and when I looked on a map I saw that his mission was not far from my house on Soi 51, though socially they were worlds apart. Kitty, for example, had never heard of the neighborhood where Maier lived, which in Thai is called *Jet sip rai*. If you asked cabdrivers on the tonier end of Sukhumvit to take you to *Jet sip rai* they would sometimes blankly refuse, shaking their heads in a certain way which seemed to imply that the words themselves encouraged mugging, mutilation, and worse.

I was invited to a party one night at Father Joe's house. *Jet sip rai* lay on the far side of the Klong Tuey walls, and I rode there on a hired motorbike. The gate by the railway track had an English sign: WELCOME. It was touching when you considered that not a single tourist had ever been there. It was four o'clock, and Father Joe wanted to show me the peculiar forest that lay near his mission, hemmed in by the wall. And of course it was the same place I had been long before with McGinnis.

Father Joe met me at *Jet sip rai* with his assistant John Purdoe, a New Yorker. It was a study in contrasts. Purdoe was delicate of build, with a shaved head, quiet and warm.

Father Joe was large of girth, in a Hawaiian shirt, motile with a bustling, restless, up-for-a-lark intelligence and delicate pale skin as quietly intimidating as scholarly parchment. And it's rare that one is intimidated by a man's *skin*. He talked loud, however. In Thai, English, Lanna. He spoke them all. Like a Pied Piper, children swarmed around him, tugging at him, demanding things, beseeching in the way that only small children can. They had AIDS.

"You look like a tourist," he said very loudly (slight Chicago Irish brogue?). "A tourist from Bangkok, I'd say. Wouldn't you, John?"

For there are two cities when seen from the perspective of *Jet sip rai*. Klong Tuey and Bangkok.

After the kids had been shooed back into the Catholic hospital, the three of us went for a short drive in Father Joe's car. The windshield was emblazoned with the word SANCTITY. We got out at the edge of the forest and began walking with long, purposeful strides. One shouldn't look aimless in a place like this. A dirt road ran alongside the Klong Tuey wall and to one side of it was the forest. Gangplanks led back into the jungle, which is to say into dark and leafy confusion. And there were rivers of trash that had *curves* and banks, mountains of garbage where half-naked men stood in the dawn light covered in "five Buddha" tattoos.

At a clearing, a small mob of skeletons came pouring out of the trees, begging for money. They were unafraid of our whiteness, or of the authority of a priest. It was a bizarre ambush. There was nothing in their eyes; the motor reactions of their limbs were unhinged, so that they walked like epileptics. Their backs and chests were tattooed with "nine crowns" motifs, magic Buddhist talismans.

It was obvious that Father Joe kept them alive in some sense; he provided a steady trickle of small handouts. For a moment the mood was tense as the demands became slightly threatening. Father Joe went on tiptoes to make himself fractionally taller and spread out two large hands filled with twenty-baht notes. The mob grabbed at them and Purdoe whispered in my ear, "I think we should get out at this point. It's getting a little weird." But it also struck me that Father Joe's almsgiving—the actual danger of it—was a sign of his character that went well beyond piety or duty. There was a look of love in his face.

Farther into the forest, there were paths made of compacted rubbish, glass, and cardboard, paths beaten down by bloody bare feet which had left their traces on it. At the bases of the trees stood sinister red shrines packed with votive candles and Barbie dolls and playing cards. Where the dead are, there are shrines, even if they are nailed together by addicts.

We came to a clearing, and Father Joe mopped his brow with a handkerchief. It was almost a hundred degrees and airless. He seemed happy with the giving away of money, the dispersal of the desperadoes, and the fact that they hadn't followed us with meaner intentions. It was a calculated risk every time he came here, unprotected and padded with cash, but I suppose they knew he would give it all away anyway. For Father Joe, it was just another day of love. A "ride on the wild side of mercy," as he calls it.

"Well," he said, smiling, the freckles on his forehead shining through beads of sweat, "shall we go to the party?"

•

Father Joe's house lies at the back of the Catholic mission, which is removed from the streets of *Jet sip rai* by a series of metal barriers and walls. It is funded by Canadian and American patrons at some cost, and is finished with solid stone and teak. To get there one has to walk through the school and the hospital, and since it was still light I could see the AIDS wards where a group of visiting Mormons based in Bangkok were playing Thai pop songs to the patients, making them clap along. I went up and had a look, immediately stiffening with anti-Mormon rage. It was certainly an incongruous sight, the apple-faced young Americans brimming with animal vigor, and speaking perfect Thai, belting out songs to a roomful of emaciated AIDS victims who looked on with a stunned admiration that could not quite decide on an appropriate reaction. A couple of the Catholic administrators looked on as well, exchanging mildly skeptical glances. It must have had something to do with the funding system. After a song, one of the boy singers held up his hands and said in beautifully supple Thai, "Okay, folks, we came to tell you all about the Lord Jesus. If you liked our songs, hopefully you'll like our message!"

So we went up to the roof, where a mountain of diapers donated by an American company lay waiting to be claimed, and where lovely small children—the AIDS orphans—spun like tops through the corridors, *wai*-ing respectfully to us as they passed. On the ground floor, the classrooms were lit up and there were classes for little girls in the classical dance form known as *khon*. Purdoe told me that one or two of them had been bought for cash by the mission from sex traders in Pattaya, but that in general the sex trade was not the source of the problems they had to address: it was mostly drugs. Bar girls in Bangkok came mainly from the north, whereas most of the women they took in here were local, and most of them were not prostitutes. Nevertheless, Father Joe had gone down to Pattaya to buy those two girls. They had a special importance for him.

•

The main room of his house was opened to the sky by large sliding French windows. An exquisite statue of the Virgin Mary, probably antique Italian, stood on a rosewood table near the stairs, surrounded by candles. There was a Thai buffet, piles of mortadella, and marinated olives. Magnums of Yellow Tail wine stood on the tables, where frail nuns and aid workers devoured plates of spiced peanuts.

I have never known any priests in my life, not since I was a child, so I was not sure what to expect in a priest's house. Especially a priest's house in Bangkok. But in a single moment all my memories of my own Jesuit schools came back, and above all the slick energy that certain kinds of hedonistic and cultured Catholic priests have. And how, for that matter, can you be truly cultured and *not* hedonistic? The question is only where the more tortured Catholic consciousness fits into this. Christianity is not exactly famed for its good living.

Father Joe seemed to believe that the world has not been created in order to be ignored. He liked to do a kind of conga dance with his young Thai volunteers, a glass of wine in one hand and a drug-addiction report sheet in the other. He whirled around his large, pretty room with his burnished red Irish cheeks and formidable width, and it was moving because you could sense that he had staked everything on his adopted life here. There was no going back. He had come to Bangkok in the sixties, the typical idealistic priest, and had lived with hill tribes in the north of the country, learning Lanna dialects, before coming to the port slum where the mazes of wooden houses were often swept by immense fires and the government seemed to be waging war on its own people. He built his own house, living for years in a field by the port wall. But where did his jollity come from? Father Joe threw grapes into his mouth, cocking his head back. The summer-grass eyes sharply assessed everyone present, making rapid notes to themselves. The social workers present talked about the *yaa baa* and *sii qun roi* in the slums. Finally Father Joe rolled back on his own sofa, took a large swipe at his wine, and seemed to consider the social complexities of getting stoned on ground-up mosquito coils.

"In 2003 the Thaksin government launched a crusade against *yaa baa* across the country. It was probably the most violent antidrug crusade on earth while it lasted. Thousands of people were gunned down by the security forces—literally thousands. But most of the factories are now across the border in Myanmar, so there was little chance of stopping it. It's like any trade: put Third World producers in with affluent middle-class consumers and you have a perpetual bonanza. The logic is unstoppable."

I sat on a sofa next to an Australian nun called Sister Joan who ran a shelter for homeless children deep inside the Klong Tuey slums. She lived there alone, with a computer, a radio set, and precious little else. What a strange life, I thought, half admiringly. It was a voluntary crucifixion of sorts, a canceling out of one's own self and its petty ambitions. But she was the merriest person I had met in years, and there was high intelligence there, too. She explained to me that she had spent all week fathoming the Thai verb "to embezzle." It was one of the most useful verbs in *Jet sip rai*, with hundreds of subtleties to master.

On the table in front of us was a Red Bull can with a burned tinge to the metal and a straw popping out of the top hole. Had it been left there to stimulate pertinent conversations or simply forgotten after a previous night's conviviality? No, said Sister Joan: earlier in the evening Father Joe's assistant had been talking to the volunteers about new drugs. And one of those drugs was 505. Five-oh-five, she explained, was made from paint thinner with a popular glue called 3-K.

"It looks like molasses," she went on. "You put it in Red Bull cans and sniff it."

"Really? Have you done it?"

"Well, I had a whiff."

The smile was shy, but by no means prudish.

"When you are done here," she went on, "why don't you come home with me and I'll show you how I live in Klong Tuey? I've been here for years as well. Father Joe and I must be two of a kind."

As Father Joe flipped sides of beef on the outdoor barbecue, I asked him if he had come to Bangkok out of an urge to discover a family for himself. It was another way of asking if love had been the driving need behind his migration to the most dismal part of what was then an unknown city.

"Love is the source of everything we do, I would say. Even if we are not aware of it. Bangkok, for me, was a way to find it, if that's what you are asking."

"It is," I said.

•

Sister Joan and I went down a path in the shadow of the
port wall, to the far side of which arc lamps and welding
crews lit up the acres of containers. On the other side of the
track, shelters rose from the jungle. People came out of
the long grass to ask for money, apologetic as lepers, and
Sister Joan dropped them hundred-baht notes as we slipped
past. Old mango trees, spreading far around themselves,
were tied up with assortments of ropes and cables, and under
them the motorbikes and hammocks were lined up in a
shade which during the day must have made the sun almost
bearable.

The houses were crammed close together so that sometimes one almost had to turn one's body sideways to slip
between them. In her denim skirt and sturdy sandals, Sister
Joan looked like a small tank from behind, and the flashlight continued its comforting swing. "On patrol," I
thought. And I speak as a lapsed Catholic. Everywhere she
appeared she was greeted in familiar terms. Planks ran
between the shacks now, the mud below a sea of syringes
and trash. Through the glassless windows we could peer
into little alien worlds. In one house a man bred fighting
cocks. There was a deer skull with fully grown antlers
pinned to one of its vertical beams. The owner sat in a corner, brooding until the flashlight stirred him and he blinked.
The animals were kept in wicker cages partially covered
with pieces of deer skin. We stopped and Sister Joan reached
up to caress a bundle of severed chicken claws nailed to a
post. Above it stood a Virgin mounted on a crenellated
pedestal.

Her house stood on one of these alleys. We went into a small, neatly arranged room that served as a living room for an elderly lady living by herself. I felt at once its gripping sadness. On a corkboard I noticed a list of Thai phrases written next to their English equivalents: "to embezzle," of course, "to pay the debt," "masseur needed." There was a simple shelf of books: *A People's Guide to the Breviary*, Cheryl Benard's *Veiled Courage*, that kind of thing. Photographs of nieces and nephews, cliffs and billabongs left behind, a beach, a faded couple who must be the parents. A life telescoped into a single room, which is what happens at the end. And yet the house was full of signs of courageous activity. A computer, files, spectacles, dictionaries, for the missionaries had to speak fluent Thai. It was a hub of purposeful activity, of quiet organization and intensity. And Sister Joan herself was the very antithesis of sadness.

I forget what we talked about. The slums, the tough-luck stories, the broken families. I asked her about Australia, because I am always curious as to how a person leaves behind a homeland and adopts another—I have done the same thing my whole adult life. But, as with Father Joe, I had not reckoned on the quality of love which must have surrounded her in this place, making it "home." A mutual dependency, too, a reciprocal need. More vulgarly, because I am not a nun, I felt acutely sorry for Sister Joan, who would soon be lying upstairs in the heart of Bangkok reading *A People's Guide to the Breviary* while half a million foreign men partied the night away around her. But Sister Joan probably felt sorry for me as well.

She came out with me to light the way with her torch, her white hair sticking up like the crest of some strange and sympathetic reptile, and I shook her hot hand. She seemed to suffer in the heat.

"Be careful going through the forest," she said. "And don't give the addicts any money. Unless they threaten to kill you, of course."

I got a lift with John Purdoe back to Sukhumvit, and in the car he told me why he, too, was exiled in Bangkok, though he had never expected to be. A Jewish boy from Brooklyn working closely with a Catholic priest in a Buddhist slum in Southeast Asia.

"I just wish sometimes I could talk to someone about Isaac Bashevis Singer. I wish I could talk to someone who's actually *heard* of Isaac Bashevis Singer. But who can I do this with? There's no literary culture here. It's embryonic. It's the one thing that bothers me. One has to do without that."

At this very moment, a bike shot by with two Thai girls perched behind the driver. It was lightly raining and they held two banana-colored umbrellas above their identical haircuts. As they glided past his window they shot John a declarative, sultry, all-the-sex-you-want smile. For the scholarly-looking boy from Brooklyn, it was enough.

"And then *that* happens. You get that come-hither look. Spontaneous, for no reason, just like that. Woman to man. No, no come-hither looks in Brooklyn. That's what keeps me here, apart from the work with Father Joe. The come-hither look. It makes your day. Perhaps you find that foolish."

"Not at all. It's like being surrounded by opened doors. You aren't going to walk through them, but they're open all the same."

"Exactly. It makes you feel alive. Here, you *are* alive.

This is the most alive place on earth. Even if it doesn't have Isaac Bashevis Singer. And even if our women wouldn't understand in a million years."

Wouldn't they, though? I have met plenty of *farang* women who love Bangkok precisely because it's the only city in which they are not constantly harassed. No one even looks at them. They can wander the three-a.m. bars with total anonymity, impunity, for once in their lives reduced to the status of sexual ghosts. As for the Gloria Steinem brigade—well, what was the point of even trying? There was no pleasing them about anything. They were not inclined to really consider the question of sex as anything but a problem of crime. And I thought of all those "hard-hitting exposés" you see in Bangkok Airport about the sex business, consisting of interviews, economic analyses, and political laments, and I wondered why I never found this type of enquiry particularly enlightening. Perhaps because it contains so few surprises. Perhaps because we are invited so crudely to disapprove and to wring our hands.

"And, anyway," John said wearily, "life is elsewhere, and we all know it. There's nothing to be done except live, and that's what we do anyway."

I replied that it was a sentiment which I always appreciated hearing, because it was unanswerable—that, and subtly optimistic.

•

During the spring months, if "spring" is a word that can ever apply to a tropical monsoon climate, I found myself drifting in a wet heat akin to the inside of a *bain-marie*. I discovered an entirely new color which could be called "tropical monsoon," the seething dark-gray hue of a warm-water seal's coat.

I often went wandering through the neon of Wireless Road or the electronics market at Pantip Plaza—a fine place to stroll around at night because it retains the energy of daylight hours. I went there to buy CDs and electric razors and gadgets, starting at around seven, when it was already dark. The intensity of the neons stacked around several floors stung the eyes, and the words that they projected meant nothing: *Kensington, Epson, Zest Interactive, Hardware House*. The plaza (actually a vertical mall in which the floors are stacked on top of one another) is a hip hangout for the young, who flock there at night to see and be seen.

At the top of the building hang the dismal words IT CITY. I bought a Cyberdict talking translator which could render my thoughts in Vietnamese as well as in clumsy Thai. And so to the sleek black Vaio store and the Data IT store, through aisles of optical mice and modems, through shelves of laptops and Alcott laser paper: a ghost stuck in the future. Even coming from America, wandering through an Asian electronics mart feels like being fast-forwarded years into the future.

In another mall where youth collect at night, the Siam Center—which is devoted to the cause of fashion—I noticed that the illumined English ad panels were even more textual. It was as if the present age needed to bring certain thoughts and expressions to the surface, and that these needed to be said in as aphoristic a form as possible. Like the strange assertions that might adorn a temple or church, these were lit up like holy text, and were just as enigmatic, some of them derived seemingly from classic Western literature:

Fashion is concentration on design but no concern on worrying

Fashion is black color and long hair

Fashion is new, different and appealing in any way
In everything, creation, lifestyle—*The Odyssey*

Norule Noreason

Underneath two long lines of Thai script: Time's end
These surrealist screeds excite no surprise whatsoever.
It's as if people are willingly predisposed to accept the idea
that time and history might suddenly come to an end. Does
Buddhism, in any case, much care about our idea of either?
Buddhists, ironically, might turn out to be the ideal con-
sumers, if their admirable detachment could be combined
with very fat wallets.

But it was also ironic that these screeds lit up the night in
full view of the demonstration by Siam station, where you
could say that history was reasserting herself in no uncertain terms. Yet those clean, white labyrinths did possess
an unnerving impassivity which made them calm—and I
thought of Charcot's chilling phrase *"Le beau calme de
l'hysterique."* The beautiful calm of the hysteric.

It could be a new kind of modernity. Outwardly deriva-
tive of the West's, but different at its core. This was why it
seems to consist of pastiche and unconscious parody, misunderstood borrowings and vacuous reproductions. Its reality
is somehow hidden.

Perhaps it's the habit we have of thinking that much of

the world is a reproduction of ourselves, of America, when it is obviously nothing of the sort. The West is no longer ascendant. "America persists in identifying modernity throughout the world in relation to itself," the philosopher John Gray has written, "at a time when in East Asia modernization is advancing swiftly by repudiating or ignoring the American model. The very idea of 'the West' may already be archaic— the old polarities of East and West do not capture the diversity of cultures and regimes in the world today." A diversity, he suggests, which makes "the interpenetration of cultures an irreversible global condition."

•

I was sitting one night at a café inside the Siam Center called Bluecup Coffee and Tea. I was on the verge of losing my hearing at the hands of pounding techno music as I tried to read a volume of Jerry Hopkins, when I saw a *farang* whom I thought I knew slip past in the human stream. It was already fairly late, and I was about to leave anyway, so I followed him out into Siam Square. As he cleared the glass doors of the mall, I came up behind him and examined with great interest the lightweight brown overcoat he was wearing, since no one wears an overcoat in Bangkok, however lightweight it might be. He had spiked hair and wore cracked English shoes, quite elegant; he walked like someone who has just broken a plate-glass window with a brick, his head shifting quickly from left to right, shoulders a little hunched, quick paces. From whom would a *farang* have to hide in the world's most brightly lit commercial plaza? And from where did I recognize those irritable, shy, darting mannerisms? Then, as I noticed a spot of yellow paint on the hemline of his coat, and registered how strangely crumpled it was, I knew that it must be the Spaniard from all those years before at the Primose, in Wang Lang. "I know your name," as Oscar Wilde had it, "but your face completely eludes me." Unsure what to do, I followed him to the road under the Skytrain tracks, where he stopped to hail a cab. I stepped in front of him and said, "Helix?"

His face was exactly the same, only hardened a little. But he didn't respond to the name, merely raising his eyebrows.

"I am Acevedo," he said icily. "Are you a client?"

"A what?"

This made him relax a little while he scrutinized my face for signs of familiarity.

"Do we know each other?"

His hand was raised, a cab slowed for him.

"The Primrose," I blurted out. "You're a painter."

Now his brows tightened. Ah!

"Felix," I said apologetically. "Isn't that your name?"

"Then why did you call me Helix?"

"It was a slip of the tongue. Apologies."

He looked at me warily. "It's Felix, not Helix. Helix is not a name."

"Of course not, of course not. Do you remember me?"

"I think. We used to call you The Transatlantic."

"The what?"

"The Transatlantic. It was a nickname."

Suddenly all was smiles and how-are-you's. But should we embrace even though we had never exchanged a word before?

"I see," he said, opening the cab door. "So we should talk about old times, no?"

"Are you busy?"

"I am just going home to have a drink. I live at the Plaza Athenee."

"You *live* at the Plaza Athenee?"

"I have a deal with a client. A year at the Plaza Athenee. Free."

I got into the cab after him, and I thought, "The Transatlantic? Is that what those bastards called me behind my back?"

•

How strange to re-find the *mierda* man, who used to hurl glued birds onto his canvases. He had grown up a bit in the intervening years. Embarrassingly, I now had to reckon with the enormous fact that I knew nothing about him at all. In the event, it mattered little since we had a few characters in common and could engage in some affectionate retroactive gossip.

"Why," I asked in some irritation, "did they call me The Transatlantic?"

"Well, it was because it was felt you were a bit like an ocean liner which doesn't seem to come from anywhere in particular and doesn't seem to be going anywhere in particular. And no one could really nail down your accent. McGinnis said you couldn't be English. He said you sounded like a phony American."

"That bastard."

"I'm sure he didn't mean it badly. You were like a mystery to us. A nowhere man, like in the Beatles song."

"I'm not a nowhere man. And I don't have a transatlantic accent. I'm British to the core. Unfortunately for me."

"Well, there you are, then. I am Spanish to the core, unfortunately for me."

It was inconceivable to me how someone could actually live for a year in a suite at the Plaza Athenee, nor what he would have to do to earn this extravagant privilege. It was better not to ask. It's a beautiful hotel, perhaps along with the Peninsula the most beautiful in the city, and on its roof there is a wide pool with a Thai pavilion, luxuriant tropical trees, and some sly, upper-end girls. At this elevation, the city recedes slightly and alters its aspect. You are within a forest of blazing skyscrapers next to the Four Seasons Place, a brutal corporate set piece of "mixed use" intentions, with residential and commercial windows juxtaposed. There is a curious connection here between luxury and elevation, a *rising above* the city. A connection between height off the ground and social class. Felix ordered us drinks and soon we were almost alone by the pool, with the rasping cicadas that clung to these desperate urban trees. He peeled off his ridiculous overcoat.

"I come here every night for inspiration."

He looked a little tired, and more than a little old. A lifer.

"Are you working on any projects in Bangkok?"

"I've never worked in Bangkok. I've never done a thing here. I do hotels in Indonesia mostly."

"You mean you didn't paint the mural of Alexander the Great in the Portofino restaurant in Bumrungrad Hospital?"

"The what?"

"Or that thing in the Shangri-La Hotel?"

"I've never set foot in either place. I did a resort in Lombok. Perhaps you've been there—it was sort of Islamic in inspiration—"

"Lombok?" I murmured. And all these years—

Felix was a total egotist. He had virtually no interest in

other human beings except insofar as they either crossed his path or served some immediately useful purpose to him. It is a characteristic of people who have only half succeeded, or who have not succeeded at all. The ego desperate for advantage, for recognition, for *air*. It can be forgiven in a twenty-five-year-old, or even—at a stretch—in a thirty-year-old. But at thirty-five and up? At that point it hardens into something more rancorous and irremediable. So here was Felix, who had once been "brilliant," who had dabbled in Asia as his career in Europe declined, for of course he could make far more money here than in any European city. Asia is more capitalist, more geared toward fast turnovers. Moreover, here the declining career, the accumulating slights, and the general all-around dead-endness of the artistic life would be virtually invisible. Thais couldn't parse *farang*s that finely. For men like Felix, it was all a useful subterfuge, but such manipulations could never be mentioned in polite company because, like McGinnis and Dennis, he played a Janus game with his hosts. There were separate cards, names, manners for his Thai patrons and connections. It was schizophrenia as a way of life. But, then again, it was enjoyable, exciting. Every man wants to be a bit of a Felix Krull if he can get away with it. Time's end, indeed.

The problem with this mode of exile is self-respect. One has to reconcile many things inside oneself. Bangkok was filled with guys who played in unknown rock bands, ran bars, designed hotel toilets, but among them the fires of genuine ambition were not necessarily extinguished. Because he didn't listen, Felix assumed I was a Bangkok lifer like himself. Therefore he needed to ask me if I thought my talent was being nourished here.

"I'm not sure I have much talent," I replied, quite truth-
fully as it happened. "And if I did have some, I wouldn't go
around talking about it. I come from New York, where
everyone does that, even if they have no talent whatsoever. It
makes me want to vomit. I think I came here to escape
exactly that."

"I see, I see."

But Felix didn't see. Self-deprecation was not his thing.
He couldn't quite believe in it. A great artist must have a great
ego. Olé! Self-deprecation was an admission of inferiority.

He gulped down his Sex on the Beach, and his lips were
very shiny.

"I feel that no one understands me. I am alone. They
nod, they pay, they say nice things. But they don't get it."

"What don't they get?"

"They don't get art. They despise it, but they're too
bourgeois to admit it."

"Perhaps," I thought sadly, "they get it all too well."

"Well, I guess that makes me a nowhere man, too."

He didn't mean it, but he grimaced. The shadows of
bikinied girls moving among the trees consoled him,
because, after all, it was the great consolation of this city. I
wanted to ask him about the dead birds, because I had
thought of it many times over the years, but now I was sure
it would needle him. He gestured at the pool meanwhile,
at the Thai pavilion and the high-wattage panorama, and
sighed: "It's not so bad. I can deal with this." I merely asked
what his Indonesian hotel art was like.

"Birds, mainly. I do seabird motifs, pelicans, parrots,
macaws. The tropical species. It works great in bars and
lighter-end cafés. Sometimes I do a shop or two. You know,

hotel boutiques. It makes them cheerful, lively. Birds have that effect upon us, you know. They cheer us up."

"Do they?"

"Oh yes. They make us feel close to nature. You know, movement, chatter, color. Gaiety. They have psychologists studying it for the hotels."

"Who would have thought it?"

"One day I am going to do one big fucking mural in Bangkok. The best in the city. All birds. A vast collage of toucans and albatrosses. People will be completely amazed. It'll be in all the guidebooks. I've been talking to the management team of a new hotel owned by a Sikh millionaire. They love my stuff. Felix, they say, you've got the touch. It's like a helix, you see. You know what a helix is? Like a structure that stands by itself, elegant and airy, and it can be full of holes but it still stands up. It's like DNA. That's a helix, too. It's right in the heart of nature, man; it's what nature is all about. Structures, no bullshit."

"Well," I said, "I should probably get going before I get too drunk."

"No, no. You got to hear this bird mural idea out. We're already planning it. It's going to be a huge, mysterious beach somewhere in Patagonia. No humans, just a killer whale in the background. They're thinking it'll be rocking for the underground nightclub. On the beach—a moon and a sun, both night and day—"

His hand swept through an arc, like a little palm-shaped sun. I looked at my watch with as much emphasis as I could muster.

"—and then on the black sand a great congregation of tanagers and hummingbirds. An ornithologist's dream. Or nightmare. The age when the human race has died out and only the birds remain. You know, like Hitchcock."

I got up, and he got up as well. Oh dear, I thought.

"That's a radical vision," he added heatedly. "The Thais will definitely freak out."

"They will, Felix. I'm very glad to have run into you again. Time does fly, doesn't it?"

We walked to the elevators.

"That's another of my metaphors," he said excitedly.

"What is?"

"Time flying. On wings. Like albatrosses."

"I suppose it would be."

"You should come and see my suite."

"Leave me your number," I said, hurling myself at the elevators. "It's a small city for us *farang*s. Everyone knows everyone."

But this was not at all true. It was a very big city and most *farang*s did not know each other, and never would.

"If you ever go to Lombok—" he began.

There is always that moment when a man in an elevator stares at another man whom he will never see again with a superhuman coldness. Their gazes cross like sabers, not in anger but in exasperation; there is a mental *clink*, the sound of fine steel clashing. I felt it with Felix. He now took a half step forward. He held up one hand as if to stop the departure of the elevator for a moment and leaned toward me, whispering. His face went suddenly red and his eyes took on a more piercing clarity.

"Wait a minute," he said, balancing on one foot as he held the door open and looked quickly over his shoulder. "Before you go, can you lend me forty dollars?"

During the first months of summer, I began traveling again, to Laos, Malaysia, and Cambodia mostly, profiting from that tiresome monthly duty known to all expats as the "visa run." Thailand obliges all its temporary residents to renew their visas at the end of every month. Sometimes I went to Macau for the weekend and holed up at the Hotel Lisboa to play the all-night baccarat tables. Since numerals in Thai and Cantonese are virtually the same I could place my bets without the assistance of a translator, and thus lose as much money as I felt I could.

There was something comfortingly integrated about an establishment where you could sleep, eat at a Robuchon restaurant with a wine list furnished by its billionaire owner Stanley Ho (if you could afford it), and gamble till dawn among Mongolian prostitutes as stately and cold as galleons bristling with heavy guns. Looking out my window, I was struck by how much like Bangkok Macau was becoming. The whole place was being taken over by Vegas moguls. A Sands Casino had just opened by the ferry terminal, and the night sky was already a jigsaw of neons devoted to the selling of baccarat and sex.

"The American," Hemingway once said, "is a lonely killer." But what he really meant was that the American of his age was *more* of a lonely killer. In truth, we all have a lonely killer inside us, however smothered by pious social conditioning. As soon as he is alone, a man reverts to a different modality without even knowing it. He drifts away from respectable relations with women, the marriage, the monogamous arrangement, and however much he protests to the contrary, deep down he is excited.

When I came back to Bangkok after these excursions I always felt that I was returning to the region's heart. The hugeness of the city, its advanced system of hospitality, its affluent middle class, its perfect hotels, its chaotic ease, all struck me as momentous. But what I noticed even more was something that is not obvious walking the streets but which becomes more so with time: the visibility of homosexuality.

Walk down Silom Soi 4 and you see the ease of the homosexual man in the street, the natural flamboyance of the *kathoey*. In Bangkok, male beauty is heightened to the greatest degree, and then unleashed. Neither in China nor in Malaysia, nor in Cambodia nor Laos, did I feel that same comfortableness. Here, in the playground of the street, men are restless, ruthless, atomized, but they are nevertheless comfortable; they have reverted back to themselves.

•

"It's all a question of not lying to oneself," McGinnis would say when we had dinner on Soi 4, admiring the military cops who sometimes swanned by in elongated helmets looking like hermaphroditic Egyptian priests. "I've always found it interesting to compare the behavior of gay men and lesbians, and as far as I can see, there is no resemblance whatsoever. They are poles apart. This proves that gay men are more purely male. And that the heterosexual male is a hybrid, a compromise. Partially castrated, in fact. It can scarcely be denied, can it? I am not saying we should act on it, but it's an observation."

We lay outside on a pile of cushions, eating *thord mun plaa*, fried spicy fish cakes with cucumber dip, and pomelo and pork salads laden with river shrimp. Boys traipsed by in Lakota Sioux outfits revealing their buttocks, in skirts and cutaway jeans and mink coats. There is just one hour in the twenty-four-hour cycle when a given street suddenly explodes into life. McGinnis was a highly sensitive instrument for measuring such things and his face lit up with glee.

"There, there. Feel it? Wild, eh? Shit, if you can't feel that at least once a day you're a dead man, a total dead man. All those dimwits who think this is *sordid* are on the wrong side of life, my friend, they don't understand a thing—

"Did you know," he went on, leaning back with a long, thin cigar, his old Carnaby Street antique shirt blotched with moisture, "that the word *kathoey* is actually Khmer in origin? They call them the *third sex*."

"It's funny. I don't think about them at all. And yet they set the whole tone of the place, don't they?"

"They do. I am sure more knowledgeable people would say that we two know bugger-all about Thailand, and I would be the first to agree. I know even less than bugger-all. But one thing I'm sure of is that you can't understand this city without understanding *kathoey*s. There's a whole Buddhist explanation for them which is connected to the Thais' profound tolerance within this one sphere—the sphere of love."

"So what's the explanation?"

"No idea. I'm always too stoned to read the books. Something about sinners being reincarnated as *kathoey*s, then being born again as heterosexuals. As in, we have all been *kathoey*s in previous lives."

"It's highly likely," I murmured.

"It's a mind-blowing idea that every man has been a woman in a previous life and every woman has been a man. And every man and every woman has been a transsexual. If that doesn't make you tolerant by nature, what will?"

We watched the ladyboys for a while, acknowledging even that there was sometimes something irritating about them. A showiness and hardness in the eye, and in the tilt of the pseudo-female bottoms. An ass should be female or male, somehow, but not in between.

•

The British scholar Richard Totman has explored the world of *kathoey*, and he claims that Buddhism's early *Tipitaka* canon identifies not two sexes but four. Male, female, and what it calls in Sanskrit *ubhatobyanjanaka* (biological hermaphrodite) and *pandaka* (literally eunuch, weakling; translated by the word *bando* in Thai). Thai Buddhist commentators add their own gloss, identifying *ubhatobyanjanaka*, for example, as what they call in Thai *kathoey thea*, or "true hermaphrodites," and interpreting *pandaka* to mean *kathoey*, as in "a castrated man." The Buddhist scholar Suchip Punyanuphap adds that this is "a person who takes pleasure in having relations with a man while feeling they are like a woman."

In the Theravada tradition dominant in the Lanna region of the north, there are creation myths which describe not two mythic founders of the human race—like Adam and Eve—but three. A primordial man, a primordial woman, and a primordial hermaphrodite. There is conflict between the man and the woman and the hermaphrodite, but the latter is still there in this Buddhist Genesis, even if he functions a bit like the snake in the biblical version. Napumsaka (as he is called) actually kills the heterosexual male when he sees that the woman loves him.

In his prominent 1983 dictionary, Manit Manicharoen explains that homosexuals and *kathoey*s are not the same thing, though there is an obvious overlapping. "Homosexuals," he writes, "or the sexually perverted, *wiparit thang phet*, are not *kathoey*. The characteristic of a *kathoey* is someone who cross-dresses (*lakka-phet*), a male who likes to act and dress as a woman, or a female who likes to dress and act as a man." Biological hermaphrodites are actually extremely rare, and the vast majority of *kathoey* are biologically male but psychologically female. A hundred years ago they were described as *phet thi sam*—the third sex.

"The concept of more than two genders," he writes, "would appear to have been inherent in Thai culture right through from ancient to modern times." The term *kathoey* may even be pre-Buddhist. And the cross-dresser, transgender subculture is recognized at the highest level of the Buddhist state. In the Vinaya, for example, that part of the Buddhist canon that deals with the behavior of monks, cases of monks changing sex, turning themselves into women, are not remarkable. McGinnis was right: Buddhists do indeed believe that one can be reborn as any of the three sexes, and that in fact one almost certainly already has been.

More darkly, Thai Buddhism appears to believe that people become *kathoey* because they have sinned in a previous life. They may have sexually abused their children or deserted a woman whom they had made pregnant. However, because his state is predestined, no blame falls upon the *kathoey* himself. No karmic ill accrues to either him or the homosexual whom he sometimes ressembles: neither state is seen as sinful. "Changing one's sex," writes the Buddhist author Bunmi, "is not sinful. But sexual misconduct is sinful." He is referring to heterosexuals.

•

"Have you noticed," McGinnis said as we walked up Silom, making our way through the night markets, through gangs of tourists whose faces looked as if they were exploding in slow motion, "that there is a supernatural atmosphere in the city right now, an atmosphere of cheap magic and uncanny happenings? Nothing seems quite normal. I was reading in the paper today about these mysterious tubes of silvery gelatin that keep appearing in different neighborhoods as if they were falling from the sky. Have you seen this in the papers? The *Bangkok Post* has entries on it almost every day, sometimes on the front page. No one knows what they are, though among schoolkids there is a wild Internet rumor that they are extraterrestrial in origin. Other people say that they are as yet unknown species of fish sucked by atmospheric conditions out of the South China Sea and deposited onto Bangkok. They find them quite frequently in *working-class neighborhoods*. I'm not saying that means anything, but one could suppose that those neighborhoods have a higher level of superstition. Still, many of my middle-class Thai friends are convinced there is something fishy, as it were, going on."

"I didn't know you had middle-class friends."

"What other kind are you allowed to have as a *farang*? I

except bar girls. Anyway, I have also heard that these mysterious silver objects are most likely components in the cooling
systems of hospital refrigerators. It is, you see, an elaborate
hoax, like corn circles, designed to elicit a chain reaction
among the 70 percent of the population who have no functioning brain. It's a work of art in a way. Imagine all the
trouble you'd have to go to, to plant tubes of fridge gelatin
all over Bangkok and then have it written up by some idiot
reporter at the *Bangkok Post* who, if he didn't half believe it,
wouldn't bother to write it up at all."

•

We took the Skytrain to Thong Lor and then walked all the
way back down Sukhumvit. McGinnis said that it was high
time we finally visited the Eden Club, which is located on Soi
7/1, and though I had no special desire to go I knew that I
would be dragged there all the same—and there was a side
of me, I admit, that was curious to see what this inner cham-
ber of his imagination actually looked like. But there was
time, he said, these things had to be done slowly. It was fun
to walk around lasciviously relishing what one was going to
do over the next twelve hours.

"Some of us," he said as we clambered down into the
heat of the street at Thong Lor, "are condemned to a life of
relentless satisfaction. It's tough."

The streets around Thong Lor seem like a series of draw-
ers inside which different utensils are stored for specific uses.
On the quieter stretches, we counted our way up or down,
soi by *soi*. The mood became a little more introspective as
we passed shuttered stores with votive jars outside them
ringed with ash, bowls of water upon which lotus floated

with figurines of the Girl with the Long Hair, a popular Buddhist legend. We passed Sukhumvit Shark Fins, where we often ate, with its bloodred external fans and stencils of mako sharks on the windows. And then Tulip Massage, and dusty tailors where I sometimes bought ties and cuff links, but which later struck me as being like funeral parlors with clothes suitable for the Final Day. We returned to Shark Fins and made them set up a table outside. I had a very trashy question which I had wanted to ask McGinnis all along. I wanted to know how many of these night ladies he had slept with during his interminable, irresolvable sojourn in the City of Angels. It's a vulgar question, but I was just curious. If Bangkok was a place where men could behave without strictures, how high would their promiscuity soar?

Over swimming pieces of shark fin, he came slothfully clean.

"Well, I don't keep a little black book with the tally. I am sure it is somewhere in the vicinity of a thousand three hundred, something like that. Please, if you can, desist from the mechanical lecture on AIDS. It seems, incidentally, that the AIDS vector is slowest among the prostitutes precisely because they are the only people who use condoms at all times, at least in Bangkok. Of course, nobody can give them credit for that. We need to demonize them as disease carriers. But it's true all the same. Ask any doctor in the city."

There were moments when he looked very young, flexible and reedy, the dandy on the lam. The refugee whom you could never lecture about getting a job, leading a productive life. Those things are predicated on a belief in one's future, or even the future of the race or of society. But if one doesn't have any such belief, it all falls apart.

I said, "Where are you going to die, then? Where are you going to be buried? Here?"

"I think about it a lot. I could have myself shipped back to the village of Lower Slaughter and rot there peacefully with my ancestors. It's a thick soil, very wet, perfect for rapid decomposition. I'd have a family headstone. The vicar would stop and have a look at me from time to time. Or I could be cremated here and leave nothing behind. I'd be forgotten in about a day. Actually, a day would be a long time."

Billions and billions of years to come, he added. Buddhism had it about right. There are more fearsome things to worry about than copulation.

•

At Soi 7/1, otherwise known as Soi Eden, we had a drink at a place called the Star Inn, where there was now a "Bar 24 Hours Cigar Club." The street itself was small and claustrophobic, its sooty black walls muddled with tarpaulins, sundry ladders, cracked AC units stacked up like egg boxes, rusted grilles, and ropes. In the thick heat of a hundred-degree night it was like the Black Hole of Calcutta, with girls swooning under orange parasols as they fanned themselves ineffectually, and the menu at Mike's Corner Bar offering seventy-five-baht "quiet beers" which were being gratefully guzzled by the usual ragbag collection of beady-eyed *farang*s. My skin crawled every time I moved, the glands gushing in overdrive, and I had trouble focusing on distant objects. Music flowed from every filthy crevice. In short, Soi Eden was my kind of place.

We went into the Star Cigar Club and got some Cuesta-Reyes. The place was a bit dingy, but the cool air revived.

"When we go next door," McGinnis said tipsily, and he rolled gently from side to side, "I am going to take charge, to show you the ropes. You are going to go to one of the rooms upstairs and you are going to wait there by yourself while I fix up your entertainment. It's a two-girl place, and one has to dress them with the in-house wardrobe. It's obligatory, and one is expected—if I may phrase it thus—to play *all six pockets of the pool table*. You can't do otherwise. You'll wait there and I'll send you a surprise."

"Really," I said, "it's not my thing, to be honest."

"Yes, but you are doing it *for me*, no? So I can show you how bloody repressed you are."

He turned and said to a waiter, "Two Cambodian brandies, please."

The boy flinched and stopped in mid-flight with a dainty *"Arai na krap?"* I noticed at once that he was *kathoey*, though dressed in normal monochrome waiter garb. McGinnis repeated his request. The manager came over.

"There is no Cambodian brandy, sir."

"Oh don't be ridiculous. I had it last time."

"Impossible, sir."

"All right, scorpion vodka."

"No have, sir."

We got some Johnnie Walker instead and began to drink in that steady, cool way that determined barflies have when they are embarked upon a plan of action. We agreed that we would leave Bangkok the next weekend to visit Farlo; and tonight we would stay on Soi Eden until we could stand it no longer. At about nine we moved on to the Eden Club, whose narrow and rather shabby façade rose behind a black sign with gold letters. Outside sat a cohort of pretty scary-looking molls of the hardened and uncomplicated variety. No matter. McGinnis whisked us into a dark, faintly depressed bar area with a partially mirrored wall and a smattering of green stools.

"Is Marc here?" he said to the mama-san.

The French owner wasn't in, she replied, nor was Bruce, the manager. She handed us two plasticated menus with all the services and prices listed in a matter-of-fact way. At the very bottom it was noted that "You are here for pleasure, not to drink." The set time was ninety minutes. All "accessories" were included.

"Accessories?" I whispered into McGinnis's ear.

"Every girl comes with her black box."

"A black box?"

The mama-san smiled with treacled scarlet lips and two dozen girls formed lines for our inspection. We were the only clients, apart from a wiry, potato-white German guy in a tattersail jacket and blue canvas shoes who sat on one of the stools like a predatory insect and glared at the vertical yellow line that divided the brick bar into two halves. A corset dangled from it. All those standing to the left of the line, mama-san explained, were amenable to anal sex. The German nodded sadly. McGinnis flashed his VIP membership card and then asked her to let me take the top room, number 69. When the matter was settled, they told me to go up by myself. "Your uniforms," she said to him, "have arrived." McGinnis settled in for a drink with the German, whom he seemed to know vaguely, and I went up to room 69, past doors behind which bacchanalia of various sorts were in progress. The truth is that I have always felt ambiguous about bars, clubs, and resorts, because their contrivances seem overdone and stifling. Instead of roaming the savannah, one is inside a cage. I climbed up to number 69 with both dread and arousal, perhaps a mixture that punters here relish. Inside, the room contained the largest bed I had ever seen, two king-size affairs slammed together to form a kind of sexual football pitch. The enormous shower contained four heads, like the bathroom of a gym.

I sat on the bed and waited. I was curious more than anything. I could hear the street far below, inviting me back to its more normalized excitements. Perhaps twenty minutes went by, and presently I was sure that I could detect the rumbling sound of McGinnis's laughter emanating from a room lower down the stairs. I was sure it was him, and I considered with relief the possibility that he might have forgotten all about me. My exit might be a little awkward, but it would still be blameless in the eyes of the management.

After what seemed half a lifetime a sound of feet on the stairs roused me. There was a knock on the door, and then two small girls dressed as traffic cops came in, their thick leather belts jangling with handcuffs, whistles, and plastic pistols. They announced their names, and although I was used to the fanciful names of Bangkok working girls—girls called Air, Pinky, Gift, Sand, and Ma—the fact that my *teerak* were called Bum and Cartoon did not make it any easier. The one called Cartoon strode into the room with a cheeky grin, laid her black accessories box on the bed, and put her hands on her hips.

"You go me!" she shouted in English.

"I what?"

"I go you. You go us."

Bum was close behind. "You go me. We go you."

"I'm going," I said.

Their faces fell and they became stern. Cartoon pointed at the bed, then at the box, from which she withdrew a vibrational instrument of some kind.

"Me go you here, now."

And she took out her manacles as well. Bum followed her lead, and soon they were armed to the teeth.

"You go Cartoon," she said, "then Bum."

It became a curious mime as I edged my way carefully toward the door. Yes, they were smiling and winking, but who knew if a rejection would insult them and make them cry out to the mama-san for *farang* reparations. I wasn't in the mood, and that was all there was to it. Of course, I could follow in the illustrious footsteps of Miller, Sade, Houelle-becq, and make up a scene of riotous clarity, with all the vignettes filled in with detail. But as we danced around each other, and Bum and Cartoon shook their manacles at me menacingly, I felt myself ebbing away. My ruthlessness disintegrated and I began to see all too clearly how this would look to a third eye. Sex depends on secrecy, on *only you* being the pornographic eye. Whereas suddenly I was being looked at by two cops in drag and I began to feel bored. It was not the fault of the Eden Club, still less of the adorable Bum and Cartoon. It's just that there comes a moment when the whole thing turns on a dime and the wings of desire are clipped by an unknown hand. One fades out. One wants air, sunshine, flight. And so, with a certain sorrow, a feeling of confused regret, I said goodbye to the surprised officers of the law, and fled.

In my garden house I slept through the rains of summer. And how many summers had I been in this city? Nine, ten—two? August is a month of constant lightning, of afternoons massive with cloud. The city sulks under glooms and sudden monsoons. Downpours, which Thais call *fon-tok*, and squalls that break the heat for a short while.

I dreamt I was lying with a girl on a river beach, painting her body with a fine calligraphic brush dipped in dark-green paint. It is like the story in the Japanese film *Kwaidan*, in which the blind boy is painted with spells by a Buddhist monk to protect him from ghosts. I have that image of Buddhism, for some reason: the human body covered with tattoos and spells, with writing. I remembered the addicts in *Jet sip rai*. I wrote some banalities—*I love you so very much*—but it didn't matter that they were trite. An intense emotion came with the spelling out of words on a woman's collarbone, unfolding long sentences along the space between her breasts. I recognized the woman, too; she was American. She was someone I had lost. When I woke, the rain slashed the long windows. The gardeners peered at me from under their wide-brimmed hats now serving as little gutters. I thought, "Maybe it's time to leave now. Maybe it's enough."

One day an e-mail came from Farlo, singing the praises of country life. But in it he wrote, "Have you ever been to the Iron Palace?" He said he was coming into town in a few days and that we should meet up there—it was a small temple near the Golden Mount which no one ever went to. Ay, I could hear him tut in his Dundee twang, the Iron Palace: ye've never heard of it, and no has anyone else. Perfect!

One needs reasons to keep on loving something. But one can always go out and find them. I wondered if Farlo had read my mind on this score and thrown out this Iron Palace to me to make me *think again*. I found it on the more detailed maps, marked by its Thai name, Loha Prasat, from the word *loha*, or iron. It sat in the middle of a temple complex called Wat Ratchanatdaram, like an optical illusion which shouldn't be there.

•

I arrived early, and from the street I saw it immediately where I had never seen it before: like a gothic chapel in a dimension of its own. Its black cast-iron spires rose in a mood of Edgar Allan Poe, pencil-thin at the tips and dark as graphite. It was Farlo's little joke, and I smiled. Its thirty-seven spires represented the thirty-seven Dharma of Bodhipakkhiya—the thirty-seven virtues required for enlightenment—and it was one of three "metal palaces" in Buddhist lands (the other two, by legend, were in India).

The structure is more Burmese than Thai and consists of five concentric square towers, each taller than the next. Rama III built Ratchanatdaram in 1846 for his niece, Mom Chao Ying, but the finishing touches to the Iron Palace were made only recently. For decades it was hidden behind a movie theater called Chalerm Thai, which was eventually pulled down in 1989, finally making the Loha Prasat visible once more. Now it rises from a corner of what was once the old city, near the Theptida canal.

As soon as you venture inside it, you see that it is a *chedi*, an abstraction. The door itself is almost hidden within the maze of the larger temple, and there is rarely anyone there. The ground floor is a labyrinth of symmetrical passageways that go nowhere, and so are all the gradually narrowing floors above it. At the end of each passageway is an open arch framing a Buddha, and all of these Buddhas are identical.

It is not clear what mental state such a building is intended to produce. Sameness, symmetricality, repetition: Are they there to remind the worshiper of life's futility? It is designed to get you lost. In Europe, it would be a "folly," the sort of eccentric maze which a playful landowner would have built in one of his gardens. In the heart of a city, however, the Loha Prasat stands as a stern, relentless rebuke of some kind. There is nothing here but optical effects and a tall corkscrew stairwell planted in the middle of the structure, which soars up to the top floor, where there is a small shrine lost among the iron spires. Until you arrive there, you are bound to be disorientated within a series of patterned puzzles.

I waited for Farlo up there. Because nearly all Thai *chedi*s are white, the black metal of the Loha Prasat is extraordinarily striking. Sitting right at its highest point is like sitting in the masts of a tall ship surrounded by rigging and pirate sails.

Then I saw Farlo striding across the temple courtyard next door. He was in battle fatigues, embarrassingly enough, as if he had just stepped off the bus from Pailin. Really, I thought, he hadn't changed. He had always treated the city like a back door. He sat in that bus for three hours, twiddling his thumbs anxiously, and then he got off at Ekkamai station as if it were a part of the Cambodian jungle. Many is the *farang* who wanders about Bangkok in this spirit. Half-dressed, as for the beach or the forest. As if the city doesn't really count as a city.

The corridors of the Loha Prasat are filled with sleeping dogs which do not stir as you gingerly step over them. But now I heard them yelp as Farlo came charging into the building. Rain began to spit as he labored up the iron stair-well, whistling, singing, calling my name. Ye little bastard, where are ye?

When he popped his head up and sniffed open air again, his eyes were blue as little fossilized cornflowers and his dark, tanned skin looked so much older that I almost took a step backward. Country living, I thought dismally. We embraced among the soaring metal spires as thunderclouds spawned themselves over the city below us.

"The best place to be!" he cried. "Look at that view. And no one ever knows ye're here. I like that."

We walked around the open terrace. The dogs inside the building were still barking in outrage. What had he done to them? They had been catatonic with me.

"Can almost see Wang Lang," he said as we sat by the tiny shrine, which contained not an image of Buddha but a miniature *chedi*. "Those were the days."

"How is Cambodia?" I asked.

"Bloody wonderful. I decided I'm gonna croak there. A wonderful place to croak. Won't be long now, either."

Strange, those men one sees once every two years or so, to whom one is bound by intangible connections not forged out of everyday life. I never quite knew what I liked about this hard, bitter, self-deprecating soldier. Perhaps it was his realism. Realism is a hard thing to achieve—or, rather, it simply comes out of a tough life.

I wondered why he had insisted we meet here. Kneeling, he looked thoughtfully at one spire after another, as if they could not be figured out.

"It's a hell of a fookin' building," he sighed.

I realized that he must have been coming here for years. That it was *his place* in the city, though he himself probably could not have said why. Perhaps it had qualities that appealed to him. Austerity, mystery, hardness.

We went down to the street. Next to the temple runs Lot Wat Ratchanatda, a commercial street that crosses the Klong Wat Theptida, one of the oldest canals in the city. By this crossing there is a wide square filled with restaurants where workers from local offices sit under the dripping trees with umbrellas, eating lunch. It was filled with hundreds of young girls dressed in bright-yellow T-shirts. It was a mass fad which had appeared only in the last two years or so, this wearing of yellow shirts on Monday. It's because Monday is the King's Day and yellow is the color of Monday. Did I understand that correctly? For Farlo it was one more proof of the power of collective thinking and manias in Thai society. Everyone starts wearing yellow shirts on Monday in honor of the king and it makes them feel that they belong to a large organism like an ant colony. And meanwhile, he added, the military was preparing to take power from the elected government. As we walked along the footpath on the north side of the Theptida canal with sticks of satay, I noticed him perusing the long whitewashed wall of the temple and the strings of votive toys suspended above the water, forming webs of plastic ray guns, tractors, and dolls' hairbrushes. The far side was a row of houses with shirts on hangers, shaggy mango trees, and parasols. Trees dipped their foliage to the filthy water. Someone had long ago planted dark-green European-style streetlamps here and there, perhaps when people still arrived at the temple's back door by boat, and in the gathering gloom we wondered if they would come on, if they ever came on. The balconies, the shitty awnings, the paraphernalia of family kitchens all elided into a village-like hybrid scene, half forest, half street, in which Farlo's battle gear suddenly camouflaged him very effectively. We came to the road at the canal's far end, and it began to rain heavily. The water bubbled and hissed like something boiling on a stove top. Behind us, visible again, the Iron Temple glistened wet. Farlo gazed up at it and smiled. I had thought that, having bothered to bring me all the way to the Iron Temple, he would now invite me for a drink, or even dinner. But instead, he looked at his watch and said that he had to meet a client for his eco-lodge, a pair of clients actually, who were going to meet him at his hotel, the Dream Hotel on Sukhumvit Soi 19, just around the corner from the Westin. It was going to be goodbye for now.

"The Dream is like all hotels owned by Indian billionaires. There's a stoofed tiger in the bar, and these funny little chandeliers everywhere. But I have to go. I need the business. What about you?"

"What about you?"

"Ay, what about you? Why are ye still here?"

"In Bangkok?"

"Ay, in this place. I'd thought ye'd foocked off."

"I am hanging around," I said, to make him laugh. "I can't think where else to go."

"Ye'll lose your soul here, lad."

He stuck out a hand for a cab, and there was a series of blinding lightning flashes unconnected to thunder. The air turned jittery and people began to scurry. I wanted to say something further, elicit some explanation, or else give one. But a street on the verge of a thunderstorm is never the place. We shook hands, he winked, slapped my arm, and said, "I'll be in next month, too. I'll take you to dinner at the Dream Hotel. What a bunch of tossers."

"Be careful of that stuffed tiger."

"Ay. I shot at a real one last year. Fooker ran off."

•

I walked to the river, since all the taxis were taken, and rode across to Wang Lang in the rain. Pier 10 was crowded, as it always was, and the water plants sloshed around the corroded piles under the houses. There stood what had been the Primrose, and the Black Canyon café, and a few new places, elegant and chic café-theaters perched over the water with views across to the Grand Palace. I had not been back here in years, and all the surface colors seemed inaccurate, misremembered. Clusters of teenage girls in the yellow shirts stood around the gourmet espresso coffee bars in which Wang Lang seems to rejoice, and Indian music poured from stalls specializing in Hindu relics. The flower shops still burst with orchids and lilies, and the cosmetics stores still offered vertical boards of violently painted fingernail extensions. The covered warren of passages glowed under the storm-light falling through the same plastic, see-through ceilings. Under a nest of decayed girders, the same mannequins stood in rows, showing off cheap and sparkling dresses. The souk was alive as always, soft with its own signs, which read *Kitto*, *Adda*, *Aerosoft*, *Coffee*. I slipped past rows of cheap shoes colored like jungle flowers, those ardent pinks and creams which accord with local taste, and soon I was in the dim spaces, the claustrophobic markets smelling of croissants and boiling meat, where trays of plastic bags filled with blue-and-yellow ices sit under the watchful eyes of old women, and where spherical metal trays of *kaeng* and wing-bean salad await a mouth. One always wants to know if a place has changed faster, or more slowly, than oneself. "Has it been faithful?" one thinks.

He was a man all alone, but he was not yet a man in the street.
—*Georges Simenon*

Years ago I lived in a place called Wang Lang, though I had forgotten if that passageway—you could hardly call it a street—onto which the doors of the condo complex opened ever had a name. Of course it did. Everything has a name, but I had never asked. It was just "the street." There is always one street that is so essential that it doesn't need a name.

As the *fon-tok* came down, I found myself trawling along it now, sniffing in the industrial aromas of the hairdressing salons and the sweetness of fried doughnuts and pork crackling as familiar things that had long ago become a molecular part of me. I passed the cranky little launderette whose machines are half open to the elements, where a drinking-water machine boasts of "reverse osmosis" refreshment. No, I thought, that wasn't there. But the flea-bitten, sleeping dogs surely were. I pushed on, to the Patravadi Theater and the new cafés that open out onto the Chao Phraya. I remembered this part of the street, too. Across the street hung wires dripping with small vines or ivy. Long side streets swept away to infinity; along them, monks walked in couples, with shopping bags. I remembered a large tree flaming with red flowers. A sign hung outside the Patravadi which read:

Remember What You Have Done in 24 Hours?

I had gone over the details of this street in my mind for
years, and I had always thought that it dead-ended at a long
brick wall which closed off all further peregrinations. It
must have been that in the past I had always turned back at
the wall, afraid or uneasy perhaps, unwilling to imagine that
my compact, contained neighborhood was not severed from
the rest of the world after all. But now I saw that none of
this was true. The street carried on. All one had to do was
turn left at the wall and follow the street's winding thread. I
was extremely surprised, because it is not like me to not follow a street. Streets are like balls of twine. They can be
unrolled indefinitely. But this one I had not unwound.

It ran past a considerable whitewashed wall, obviously
that of a wat, and was entirely covered in places by old trees.
Then the temple's roofs appeared, their red, green, and gold
dimmed by violent rain, the gold *chofa*s—"tassles of sky"—
soaring upward like curved beaks. The small mauve um-
brella I had bought near the pier trembled, and I made a
mental note of the blue metal gates and the rickety wood
houses leaning slightly on their sides. To one side, a courtyard around which saffron robes hung on lines: the monks'
quarters of Wat Rakhang. And I thought, "Rakhang?" I had
never heard of it. Above the wall, I could see its dark-green
pillars and a balcony with carved rails. The façades had
irregular reticulate designs in worn wood.

Then one comes to a scruffy park taken over by vendors
crouched under a mass of blue awnings and parasols. To the
left is the river; to the right, the *chedi*s and shrines separated
from the park by a high railing. The vendors are in fact clus-

tered around a long path that leads from the temple to the river, and they are not vendors in the usual sense: their buckets of water are filled with sea worms, large frogs, catfish, and other forms of sea life which are not on sale to gourmets. They are for the pilgrims to liberate in the river.

In a pavilion set up in front of the main shrine, the devout knelt before tall orange candles and the usual metal Buddhas. Escaping the rain, a few monks sat about, playing board games with bottle tops, watching things move past them with no sense of surprise. A working-class neighborhood temple unused to making itself into a spectacle. But the largest *chedi* was covered with grass and weeds, making it beautiful, as these strange towers should be. Its concentric, angular forms bore up a tall niche inside which a faded gold Buddha stood with the metallic gravity of an armored knight in a cathedral.

How had I missed this river of life right next to me? In the pavilion, a few *kathoey*s were making merit, throwing unbelievably sultry and flirtatious looks left and right. One of them genuflected before the altar of candles, and as her ass rose up I saw the gold letters JUICY emblazoned upon it—it's a popular American brand gimmick. She lit an incense stick, prayed with great concentration, and I watched her lips move in the shade. When she had finished, I followed her out onto the crowded path of fish sellers, which was awash with dirty water, and watched her buy a catfish. The word JUICY waddled its way through the lines of fish tanks. Juicy herself was making merit. Her nail extensions were painted lobster pink, with small Thai flags articulated upon them. She was highly aware of my pursuit.

Swinging her awkward, exaggerated male hips, she

swanned down to the monastic school and the cluttered market adjoining the river. There is a small pier here and a flight of stone steps leading down into the water, like at a temple in India. The river suddenly opens out, wide and milky-pale, with wintry-looking trees on the far bank, probably exhausted by pollution. On the pier stands a curious statue of a uniformed sailor, with wide-open eyes which stare out at the Bangkok side of the river. On the steps, hundreds of pigeons mass, waiting for pickings. How Felix would have loved it.

And here was Juicy with her bagged catfish, tentatively climbing down toward the lapping waves in her stiletto heels. She opened the bag tensely, lowering it toward the water, and the fish inside did a nervous flip. Life or death? The open river or the wok?

The fish flopped out and darted into the floating plants. A great mass of them writhed there, feeding on chunks of bread which the monks were throwing into the river as well. A seething cauldron of excitable catfish, with a few liberated eels wriggling among them.

Juicy shuddered and looked up at me. She winked, and her high cheekbones, insolently powdered, her garish rouge—not to mention the word scrawled on her bottom in gold—made her into an apparition. In her I suddenly saw the *farang* men who also lived here, who were tiny moths circling a flame which she also incarnated in her way. Vulgar, beautiful, hard. The sex of someone who has no sex, who liberates catfish and who knows that she will be reincarnated as something else. A frog, perhaps, or even a man.

"*Bai nai?*" she called over.

It was at this moment that I remembered why I liked

Buddhism, despite being unable to adopt it: because there was no drama of love at its heart. Love simply didn't insinuate itself into its view of animals and people, who were seen coldly and clearly for what they are. The misery of love didn't take center stage at all. It was breathtaking, when you compared it to us, who are taught to believe in love from day one, who believe in love as a sort of birthright. We don't see ourselves as coldly as that. We think our lives are great, meaningful dramas defined by love—and of course they are nothing of the sort.

And as dusk fell and Juicy went off with a haughty, failed smile, I thought back to the rivers I loved, to the Chao Phraya, and to the East River, and they seemed all quite identical in the end. Can rivers be reborn, too? Can catfish? Cities? At the same time, it was curious that I had never put two and two together with regard to the monks embarking and disembarking at Pier 10 all those years ago; that I hadn't realized they were of course the monks of Wat Rakhang. They had been companions of a sort, but I had never thought of them as real. They had been like painted figurines of another age, and I had underestimated how *living* they were.

So I thought of them getting off the water taxis at Wang Lang in their toga-like robes in whatever year that was, holding their plastic umbrellas and mala rosaries and looking up at the lost-looking man drinking a gin and tonic on his balcony, the new arrival in their city perched on his tiny corner of impermanent paradise, as if to ask, with a certain amusement and distance, "Is that a lonely man?"